The Business side of UK Floristry

By Alan Peck and Jenny Sheppard

Published by Alan Peck Publishing

ISBN 978-1548471057

Acknowledgements

Jenny and I have had an enormous amount of help in the construction of this book. We have endeavoured to contact as many florists as possible to get their views on the current state of the industry.

The florists who have given their views are too numerous to mention but I would like to give special thanks to Lesley Nash. If everyone knew as much as Lesley about the business aspects of retail floristry there would be no need for this book.

I would also like to thank the 6,400 people who bought 'Buying and Running a Florist Shop'. Over the twelve years since I wrote that book I have been contacted by many florists and would-be florists from all over the UK. Many of these have repeatedly pestered me to produce an updated version, with much more focus on E-commerce. You will find that this has been fully catered for in this new updated version and over 100 pages of completely new material has been added.

I would also like to thank my lovely wife Olly for her help and encouragement and for all the proof reading work.

Finally I must stress that, despite all the help I have received in compiling this book, any errors are entirely my fault and my responsibility.

Table of Contents

Chapter 4
Starting a new business

Chapter 5
Sales and marketing

Chapter 6
Buying stock

Chapter 13
Deliveries and complaint handling   **235**

Conclusion   **253**

Introduction

This is not a book about the artistic aspects of floristry. This is a book about the business side of the floristry world. Whether you have a florist shop, do floristry work from home, or have an internet based designer floristry business, this book is for you. It is aimed at anyone who wants to provide any sort of floristry service for money.

Back in 2005 I wrote a book entitled Buying and Running a Florist Shop, which was aimed purely at the business aspects of a florist shop. My first wife and I had owned florist shops and while she was the artistic one who ran a team of florists, I was the one who looked after the business side of things.

I wrote that book because I realised that although there were many books on the artistic side of floristry there was really nothing that covered the business side in any detail. If someone wanted to learn how to make a pedestal arrangement or a funeral spray they could choose from a huge variety of books. If they wanted to learn how to do the books, control their costs, increase their sales or build a website there was nothing aimed at the UK florist, and there is still nothing else available today. There are a few American books which do tackle the business side of floristry but these are of very little use to anyone operating in the UK.

I wrote that first book in the year after my first wife Liz passed away at the age of 57. We had been very happily running our shop together in Cambridge. Liz had a team of eight florists and looked after all the buying, sales and make-up work. I did all the admin work, the accounts and helped out with deliveries. The shop became successful enough that we could afford to hire more staff and gradually cut ourselves back to a three-day week, leaving more time for holidays and playing golf.

Disaster struck when Liz suddenly became ill and within four months had succumbed to pancreatic cancer. Our lovely happy world just crumbled. I felt that I couldn't continue with the shop without her and quickly sold it. When the initial grief started to ease just a little bit I realised I had a huge amount of time on my hands and I couldn't just play golf every day. I wrote the book knowing there was a gap in the market and wanting to make it a testament to Liz. I also genuinely wanted to do something for a floristry trade which had given me the happiest years of my life. I never expected the book to be particularly successful but I thought it would be therapeutic to write it.

I was staggered when the initial print run of 1,000 quickly sold out and I had to order reprints again and again. It became one of the best-selling books on floristry for each of the next ten years. Eventually I decided it had become out of date and I let it go out of print, despite continued customer demand for it.

After selling the shop I had kept in touch with the floristry world by doing business presentations, some consultancy, developing online course material and continuing to sell and market the book. It was also rewarding that a number of people who had read my book contacted me to ask if I would do some consultancy work for them, usually to check out the financials of a particular business they were interested in acquiring.

Of course, life moves on and in 2006 I married Olly. We had been introduced by a friend of hers and we set up home together in Ipswich. Olly also had an interest in flower arranging and, together with a close friend, arranges flowers for their church every week.

In 2016 I was contacted out of the blue one day by a lady I went to school with, by the name of Jenny Sheppard. Whilst sitting in her doctor's waiting room, leafing through a magazine, she had stumbled across an article about me. We got back in touch with one another and talked about what we had done with our lives since those long-ago schooldays.

To my amazement Jenny had been very much involved in the floristry world. She was a very experienced florist and flower arranger, had taught at a local college and was a Chelsea gold medallist. When I saw some of her work I knew she was an absolutely top-notch floral designer. By an amazing coincidence I discovered that the lady who does church flowers with Olly every week had been trained by Jenny.

It slowly dawned on me that if we combined our knowledge and experience we could produce an updated version of Buying and Running a Florist Shop. However we wanted to produce something which wasn't only for people with a florist shop. We also wanted to help those who were providing some sort of floristry service from home and for those who had perhaps started out this way but had developed their business into something bigger.

Throughout this book Jenny and I will cover all of the business aspects of floristry in some detail. We firmly believe that the opportunity is there for just about everyone in the retail floristry industry to improve the way they run their business and, crucially, to make more money. Retail floristry can be very challenging but the business side of it really isn't rocket science.

Personally I am not blessed with the creative ability of a professional florist but my colleague Jenny is. I honestly believe that designing and creating the products sold in the retail floristry sector is the hard part. Business is the easy part and can be learnt by just about anyone. This is why I have been so frustrated by all the people I see doing the hard part very well, but not making a good living because they fail at the easy part. Believe me – I am so ham-fisted and so lacking in creativity that I couldn't make anything that could be sold in a florist shop.

I truly believe that by the time you have worked your way through this book you will be really enthusiastic about making the changes which will see your business enjoy more success and greater profitability. Both Jenny and I are totally committed to helping you succeed.

1 Deciding what you want to be

This chapter looks at:

- Working from home as a part-time florist
- Using the internet to become a floral designer
- The way the floristry industry is changing
- The traditional florist shop
- Mail order florists
- The murky world of the virtual florist

Assuming that you've had training in floristry or flower arranging and you have some real experience, you've now decided that you are ready to move forward and start to earn some money from floristry. Your experience might have consisted of practical work at college or perhaps working for someone else in a florist shop.

Home florists

For many people the first step in starting to earn money from your own work as a florist is to do floristry from home. You may have fairly modest ambitions at the outset and are perhaps making bouquets and funeral pieces for family, friends and people they have recommended you to.

Presumably you are equipped with the tools of the florist trade and have some space in which to work. You are probably working on your own and will tackle just one piece of make-up work at a time. Possibly you have workspace in a shed, your garage or even on the kitchen table. You may even be lucky enough to have a spacious workshop. Getting set up will be covered in more detail in Chapter 5.

You will need to market your services and if you aim to be serious about building up a customer base this will mean having your own website. In this day and age trying to get yourself known simply through contacts and local advertising is an almost impossible task. Again, this will be covered in detail in later chapters.

Starting out this way in retail floristry is always going to be a gradual process. Even with a good website it takes time to get yourself known but initially you will probably be working only in your own free time

Hopefully you won't be in a situation where you are desperate for sales to enable you to pay the household bills. Perhaps you are working either full or part time in another job, or most of your time may be taken up with looking after the home and family. Whatever your situation it is likely that you can ease yourself in to becoming a retail florist. For many people it is an opportunity to further develop what has become a very pleasant hobby in to something that enables you to at least earn some very welcome pocket money.

Some people who start out this way have been trained at college and may never have worked in an actual florist shop, consequently they are sometimes reluctant to call themselves a florist, preferring the title of flower arranger. The definition of a florist is somebody who purchases flowers and accessories, conditions the stock, arranges it into different floral products and sells those products. So if you are making bouquets, arrangements and wreaths etc. from home and selling them to people, then to me you are a florist.

You should be aware that it is difficult to operate any sort of formal relay service as a home florist. Even the 'florist to florist' service offered by Direct2florist states 'Homeworkers will be removed and no refund of membership will be given'. Consequently if you want to handle orders for flowers to be delivered remotely you should consider the method used in the later chapter on Relay Services.

Designer Florists

There are now a growing number of people who started as 'home florists' and having seen their sales slowly increasing decide they want to develop their business further. This can be both a problem and an opportunity.

The problem may be that the rest of your family are becoming increasingly put out by you monopolising the kitchen work surfaces with flowers, foliage, oasis and all the tools of the florist's trade. Possibly your partner would like to be able to park their car in the garage again or put the lawn mower in the shed.

The opportunity is that by upgrading your website from an inexpensive single page to an impressive 'floral designer' site, with lots of beautiful photographs of your work, you can move into a different league. This will probably mean you having to acquire more space. Maybe you can rent a garage or a small lock-up unit on an industrial estate but this is far cheaper than having your own shop.

Some people who fit in to this category market themselves as a 'designer florist', 'studio', 'floral designer' or an 'event florist'.

There are floral designers who have become very successful and although they could afford shop premises, they choose not to take this route. To many people the combination of a superb website and a cheap lock-up unit is ideal. Their customers need never see where their products are being made and anyway, much of the work for weddings and events is done on-site.

Their shop window is their website and this can give the impression they are working from a classy shop in a city centre whereas the reality is often very different. The customers communicate via the internet and telephone and if it is a large event then the 'floral designer' can visit either the customer's home, office or the event venue.

Changing times

As a home florist or designer florist you will not get any passing trade as you would with a shop but many florist shops are now seeing very little footfall. Our shop in Cambridge was large with lots of space to display flowers, do make-up work and an area to sit customers down on comfortable sofas and arm-chairs to discuss their requirements. We had plenty of storage space, offices and car parking. The problem, of course, is the cost of all that.

Sometimes at the end of the day I would look at our takings and know that we'd had a very good profitable day but there had been very few customers in the shop. Almost all of the day's takings had come from orders taken over the internet and the phones. For this reason many florists are coming to question the need for actual shop premises. The rent and business rates and all the associated expenses of a lock-up unit on an industrial estate are very different to a town centre shop.

The past ten years have seen the number of actual florist shops decline by over 10% and the profitability of most shops has been hit hard by the supermarkets. Given that the vast majority of flowers sold in the U.K. have come from Holland (regardless of where they were actually grown) and that 80% of these are now delivered to the major supermarkets, it is obvious that the flower world has changed significantly. To counter this there is no doubt that the supermarkets have helped to grow the overall market considerably.

It has become commonplace for many people to add flowers to their shopping trolley when they do the weekly shop. Whereas flowers were once seen as an occasional luxury purchase only for special occasions, for many people they have now become a regular feature around the house.

Whilst the supermarkets were once seen only as purveyors of cut flowers most of them now offer a range of bouquets. They may not be as stylish or impressive as a similar offering from a florist shop but the price is sure to be very competitive and they will suffice for many customers.

I notice that these days many people will take both flowers and a bottle of wine when visiting friends for lunch or dinner. Buying habits have most certainly changed significantly.

Most florist shops have seen a marked decline in the number of walk-in customers buying cut flowers but there are still lots of opportunities for the conventional florist shop. Many people will still want something special for the important occasions such as birthdays and anniversaries. Of course, weddings and funerals will continue to be a source of trade for the specialist florist.

When we had the Cambridge shop we took the view that rather than get mad at the supermarkets we would take the view that they had done us a favour by making flower buying much more commonplace. Although we were selling less and less cut flowers to walk-ins we were getting more and more work for special occasions.

Customers were admitting to us that they were buying cut flowers on a weekly basis from the likes of Tesco and Sainsbury but they wouldn't dream of buying their wife's birthday or anniversary flowers there. Discerning customers were spending more money than ever before on stylish products for their special occasions.

The florist shop

Having an actual shop will certainly get you a lot of visibility and credibility. There are still a lot of people who will only view you as a 'real' florist if you have a shop. This perception is changing though as people become more and more used to doing their shopping online. A growing part of the population now see a business as being really credible only if they have an impressive website which makes it very easy to buy without leaving the home or office.

What is happening to the florist shop is of course only an extension to what is happening to the high street in general. We are all aware of the seemingly ever-growing number of empty shops in our town centres. This is having a knock-on effect on the rents landlords can charge and so at least one major element of cost is reducing.

Having a real shop does enable you to display your products and expertise. Many customers who need to plan a wedding or a funeral will still like to come to a real shop and sit down with a real florist to talk through their requirements and to look at some examples of what is possible and what is currently available.

Some customers still like to visit a shop to select a variety of cut flowers of their choice instead of buying a bunch from a supermarket. They are perhaps buying them as a gift and want the packaging to look nicer than the functional cellophane wrapped supermarket offerings. Some people will use a shop to get ideas of how they can impress their dinner guests that evening.

Many people like to talk to a real florist to find out how they can really impress the love of their life. Many men will take a 'money is no object' view if they can only achieve the desired result! I loved to see my florists deep in conversation with a customer and hear them say 'shall I tell you what would really impress me?' This is usually a sure-fire way to make a much better sale and it is one of those rare occasions where a customer spends much more than they originally planned but actually feels good about it!

There will always be a need for specialist shops offering high quality products and service. You still see lots of expensive shops selling luxury goods, even though you know that what they are selling could be bought much more cheaply online. Price is most certainly not the only factor.

Whatever sort of business you have, one big growth opportunity is contract work. So many businesses, hotels and restaurants now want fresh flowers brought in on a regular basis. This is an opportunity for every type of retail florist, whether you have a traditional shop, work from home or are one of the new breed of designer florists.

There are important knock-on benefits from contract work. Businesses often want fresh flowers in their reception area and employees of that business will often ask the receptionist 'who does our flowers?' when they have a personal requirement. It is always important to develop a good relationship with the receptionist – they can be a very good source of business.

The declining number of florist shops has created opportunities in some areas. It used to be the case that if you divided the population of the UK by the number of florist shops there were approximately 7,000 people per shop. This number has increased through a combination of an increasing population and a declining number of shops.

With some careful research you can identify areas where the only florist shop in town has closed but this was perhaps due to the poor quality and offerings of that shop rather than a lack of customer demand for quality floral products.

There are unquestionably some very tired run-down shops which could be transformed by a vibrant new owner. Some of these businesses can be acquired very inexpensively and with some initial investment and modernisation can then deliver much improved profitability for an imaginative new owner.

There has always been an element of fear amongst the traditional floristry sector that the supermarkets would decide to seriously penetrate the floral market for special occasions. If they ever decided to establish a real specialist 'point of sale' offering and go for the wedding/funeral/special events market then this would be a real threat to the average florist. So far there has been little interest among the major supermarket chains to do this as it doesn't fit in with their business model.

The value of each and every square foot in a store has meant that every unit must generate significant sales to earn it's keep. It is unlikely that a specialist floral unit, staffed with real florists, could generate enough sales and profit. It is however a given fact that the retail world is always changing!

Whatever route you wish to go down the key thing today is undoubtedly the Internet and that is why so much space is devoted to this in later chapters of this book. Just as the key thing in the property sector is location, location, location the key thing in today's floristry sector is Internet, Internet, Internet. Like it or loathe it you just can't avoid it and the importance of it will only continue to grow.

Mail order florists

This type of operation is similar to the web based designer florist but targeting a much broader marketplace with standardised offerings that can be boxed and shipped to the customer. Usually they are not seeking the wedding, funeral or event sectors but offering the sort of products that are typically sold and marketed by the relay services.

One of the first major players in this sector were Flying Flowers, who were subsequently acquired by Interflora. One of the newer operators in this field is even offering a 'bouquet' which can be delivered mail-order through the letterbox. Other major players in this sector are M&S, Next and Serenata.

Like the designer florist they need a superb website and enough space for make-up work and shipping. They do not need shop premises.

In the early days of boxed delivery of flowers there was a general antipathy on the part of many customers who saw this as a poor alternative to a hand delivered product from a real florist shop.

I must say I have personally witnessed the difference on my wife's birthday. One person sent her boxed flowers from Next and the other used a local Interflora shop. The boxed delivery came in a bland cardboard box and required some effort to unpack before actually seeing the flowers. The florist delivery was an aqua-packed hand-tied delivered in a florist van and handed over by a smiling lady in an Interflora jacket. The difference in the impact was enormous.

Over recent years the boxed items have improved and modern packaging techniques and materials have ensured most items get delivered in reasonably good shape. Personally I believe there is no substitute for flowers hand delivered by a friendly person from your local florist shop. Often they will even say 'Happy birthday' or 'Happy anniversary' and even give the recipient some friendly advice on the best way to care for their flowers.

I am writing this just after Mother's Day and have just been reading a news story on MSN entitled 'M&S ruins Mother's Day for many.' The story is about numerous complaints M&S have received about boxed deliveries of flowers. There are numerous tales of woe from furious customers. Many of them

20

have posted pictures of what they saw on the M&S website and what was actually delivered. It is a horrendous catalogue of wilted flowers, poor packaging and broken vases. Not a good advert for the floristry trade, to say the least.

Despite my reservations there are businesses who have built up a healthy level of trade with this type of operation and are often using a team of relatively lowly skilled florists to make and ship large numbers of orders right across the country. I appreciate that not everyone can afford to send an up-market product made and delivered by a local florist and so the cheaper boxed alternative has a role to play.

Some of the businesses operating in this sector use unskilled people who work on a production line basis, inserting each stem in the exact place specified within the template for each product. It is not surprising they cannot achieve similar results to a skilled, experienced florist.

As with just about everything these days the success or failure of this type of business is frequently down to the quality of their website.

Virtual florists

There are some who have used the internet to create what I call a "virtual" florist shop. This is a website giving the impression of a florist shop when there are actually no premises at all.

They are effectively acting as an unofficial relay organisation with no formal links with any real shops. Sometimes they are sad individuals who operate from home and are prepared to attempt any sort of scam which will involve them in no real work and earn them money.

I certainly wouldn't advocate anyone getting into this sector of the floristry world because even if it isn't illegal it is definitely unethical and frequently downright dishonest.

Typically this is an opportunist who suckers the customer in to believing they are dealing with a reputable florist when in practice they are simply passing on orders to a real florist, typically for an extortionate profit.

I have known an operation like this take a telephone order from a customer for a £50 bouquet and then to 'relay' it to an actual florist shop as an order for a £20 bouquet. All too often they get away with this because the sender doesn't get to see what the recipient receives. When they are found out and the customer complains they don't want to know.

It can be difficult to avoid getting caught by this sort of sting as the person placing the order with the shop that has to make and deliver the product may seem like a perfectly genuine customer.

In our Cambridge shop we received so many of these types of orders that we got to know the caller's voices and simply turned them away. Often they will call every florist in town to try to find someone willing to take the order. Usually if questioned by Trading Standards they will claim that they are providing a legitimate service by locating a florist in the appropriate area.

Deciding what you want to be – Checklist

- Part time or full time?
- Renting premises or working from home?
- Broad range or niche?
- How much can you invest?
- Traditional or E-commerce?
- Customer facing or remote?

2   Searching for a business opportunity

This chapter addresses:

- Going it alone or working with a partner
- Leasehold vs. freehold
- Location, location, location
- Finding the right business for you
- Assessing the vendor
- Adjusting to self-employment

Going it alone or working with a partner

I have generally found that most florists have lots of artistic talent but this typically doesn't go with hard headed business skills. Anyone who has the talent to make beautiful bouquets and arrangements and is also a natural businessperson is truly blessed and a very rare animal.

I have to admit to having absolutely no artistic talent whatsoever. If I had thirty minutes to arrange a dozen tulips in a tank vase it would still look awful. When we had our first shop I was determined to make my first ever gift-wrapped bouquet for my wife on her birthday. She had a rare day off from the shop and I gave her strict instructions not to come near the shop that day.

One of our florists stood over me while I ham-fistedly struggled with flowers, cello and ribbon. Several times the florist suggested it would be easier if she took over but I wouldn't have it. I struggled on for a long time and eventually I thought I had made a reasonable job of it. At the end of the day I took it home, proudly presented it to my wife and said "happy birthday darling". Her face was like thunder and she replied "who the hell made this?". It was the one and only bouquet I have ever made.

What I was much better at was the business side and anything to do with money. I ran a successful I.T. business and I ate and drank numbers. This was Liz's weakness. She had never been good at paperwork, had no interest in computers and was bored stiff by budgets and spreadsheets. Over time we came to realise that we were the ideal combination to run a truly profitable and successful florist business.

I believe that every business benefits from a combination of personalities. If everyone is an optimist potential problems may not be identified until they become real problems. If everyone is a pessimist then the flair and imagination needed to continually generate new ideas and products may be lacking.

Unlike Liz I was a morning person. I like to get up early and I have lots of energy and enthusiasm for a long morning's work. Liz hated getting up in the morning and would be very quiet for the first hour or two of the day. Then she would steadily gain in energy and enthusiasm as the day went on. Often I would feel exhausted at the end of the day while Liz would decide to start washing the shop floor.

We had been worried about how we would get on as husband and wife working together day-in and day-out. As things turned out this was not a problem. Our skills and our roles were so different that they kept us apart most of the day. Whilst Liz was serving customers or doing make-up work I would be out delivering or working on admin in the office.

In the evening we loved to talk through the day's events and what we both had planned for the following day and the week ahead.

We were partners in the husband and wife sense but any two people with complementary skills can make a venture work. There are many talented florists without business skills who have acquired their own floristry business and prospered because they have had the good sense to find someone else with the right business skills to work closely with them. Conversely there are business people without any floristry skills who have been equally successful. They have taken on talented experienced florists who have also proven to be honest and trustworthy.

If you do have the artistic skills for floristry, but not the business skills then you have to think about who can handle that side of things for you. If you hire an accountant to handle your paperwork, wages and accounts etc. this will prove extremely expensive and eat a lot of your potential profit. Also my experience is that even a chartered accountant is of very limited use to you other than to handle your quarterly VAT returns, produce your annual accounts and give advice on general aspects of accountancy.

What any floristry business needs is someone who really understands retail floristry and how it should function as a business. This means understanding not just the overall operating expenses of the business but the importance of buying correctly, managing make-up work and selling products at an appropriate price that will yield an acceptable profit.

The local accountant who does the books for a variety of small businesses typically doesn't have the specialist knowledge needed to examine the efficiency of a retail florist.

The most successful florist shops I have come across have often had a real businessperson in the family. Often it is the lady of the household who is the florist and her partner is in a completely different profession that has given them general business skills, which they have been able to adapt to the world of floristry. Of course, there are other modern households where the man is the florist and his partner the businessperson. The gender doesn't matter so long as the skillsets match the needs.

If you are single have a long hard think about your family and friends and talk to any of them who may be able to help. They may not be prepared to help you free of charge but they are unlikely to cost anything like an accountant and once they learn the business fundamentals of floristry they may prove far more valuable to you and your business.

Leasehold vs. freehold

Most existing florist shops will be for sale on a leasehold basis rather than freehold. Freehold will clearly be more expensive but if you are prepared to undertake a big enough change in circumstances this can be attractive.

You may have the option of either taking over the balance of an existing lease or taking out a new one. Stamp Duty Land Tax (SDLT) is unlikely to be payable unless you are taking over a sizeable business. You can easily check this by using the calculator on the HMRC website.

Taking over the balance of an existing lease will make the purchase quicker and easier and is more likely to eliminate any liability for SDLT. The problem is it also reduces your security of tenure. This may seem only a small gamble if the freeholder can convince you that all they want is a reliable tenant, who will pay their rent on time and undertake repairs and/or redecoration according to the terms of the lease.

Many freeholders are only too pleased to continue the status quo with a reliable tenant. They enjoy not just the rental income but also the knowledge that the property is steadily appreciating in value.

Most commercial leases are 'Full repairing' meaning the tenant has total responsibility for the repair of the premises. Usually this will include a covenant that carries an obligation to put the property in to a good state of repair, even though you as a tenant may not have been responsible for any disrepair.

This can be a minefield for a new tenant and can result in some large bills for all sorts of repairs and redecoration due to general wear and tear over a long period of time.

It is often wise to commission a full building survey just as you would when buying a house. You should also attempt to limit the repairing liability by getting the landlord to rectify any defects or to at least exclude the defects from the tenants repairing liability.

Where there is a service charge to perhaps cover common areas and services then you should attempt to cap the amount of any future increase in line with inflation.

Try to limit liability to fair wear and tear and exclude damage from insured risks. Attempt to limit your liability to internal repairing only and make the landlord responsible for all other repairs. Exclude liability for 'Inherent Defects' related to problems linked to the original design and construction of the building. This covers problems that were present at the time of completion of a building but which may not be apparent in a survey.

With our second shop we took on the responsibility for an elderly, tired looking property and had a surveyor produce a 'schedule of condition' for the premises at the time we were negotiating the lease. This involved producing a detailed report on the condition of the property, including photographs of all the weak points such as damp, damaged flooring and suspect woodwork. This cost us some £600 but it gave us great peace of mind. We knew that we could use it to fight any unjust future claims when we eventually came to the end of a lease and were either negotiating a new lease or vacating the premises.

A long lease gives you the security of knowing that you will not have to find new premises for a long time but if the business takes a dive you will still be liable for the rent until either the end of the lease or until you can assign the lease to someone else. If the owner of the freehold should ultimately decide to use the premises for a different purpose you may not be able to renew the lease.

It is advisable for any prospective purchaser to find out all they can about the freeholder. We didn't do this sufficiently well when we bought our first shop and then experienced lots of problems with a rogue landlord who the police were frequently making enquiries about. With the freeholder of our second shop we had a very professional but friendly relationship and never a cross word.

In addition to checking out every aspect of the lease you obviously also have to consider the running costs of the building. Heating and lighting costs for an ageing property can be vastly different to a new-build.

The lease of a shop is of critical importance and you have to consider the total liability over the full term of the lease. If your business fails during a recession it can be incredibly difficult to get someone to take on the liability. If you fall into debt, have little income and are still legally liable for the full rent for the balance of the lease then the situation can be truly disastrous. This is how people become bankrupt.

Whatever the lease situation be sure to have it thoroughly checked over by a solicitor before going ahead and purchasing the business.

Freehold is sometimes attractive to a buyer, particularly if there is accommodation as well. Having a flat over the shop may seem very attractive in terms of there being no commuting to work but being available all the time to the staff can become a real bind. Even the keenest owner needs time off and the chance to get away from the shop at times.

Location, location, location

The location of a shop is obviously one of the most critical factors in assessing the viability and the value of the business. If you are taking over a Designer Florist business operating perhaps from a lock-up unit on an industrial estate then you only need to consider whether the rent and business rates are reasonable, the location convenient for you and that it is the right size and appropriately equipped.

With a shop the importance of the location is much more complex. A town centre location with high pedestrian footfall is always likely to generate a high volume of walk-in sales. The downside is that the rent will almost certainly reflect this. A location on the edge of town may have a much lower rent but also a correspondingly lower level of walk-in trade.

If a shop is not in a town centre then it can make a difference which side of the road it is on. It is generally considered that a florist shop will do better if it is on the 'going home' side of the road. This is because people are more likely to buy flowers on the way home, rather than on the way into town because they wish to minimise the amount of time they are out of water and possibly in the hot boot of a car.

A location right on a corner can be a problem as the busyness of the road junction can require all of a driver's concentration. If a driver is busy looking at side roads and other vehicles there is no time for taking in anything else. However, if the road is so busy the traffic is often stop-start this can be an advantage, particularly if you have your own parking area. When people are stuck in traffic they are much more likely to notice the shops on either side. Some shops on busy but free-running roads often go unnoticed, even by regular commuters.

Our Cambridge shop was on the outskirts of the city but still had plenty of walk-in trade. This was because it had good parking on it's own forecourt and overflow parking at the rear of the shop. Many customers would shop in the city centre but call in to our shop on the way home as they did not want the inconvenience of walking around town with a bouquet of flowers.

Although it is desirable to have parking for both customers and staff this is usually impossible in a town centre and deliveries by wholesalers in huge lorries can be a nightmare. I always enjoyed being on the edge of the city with lots of parking and easy access but I always knew there was a price to pay for this.

As mentioned elsewhere in this book, we found that as the years passed a larger and larger percentage of our business was coming in via the Internet, the phone and the Interflora relay system. Many florists now operate from an industrial estate, not just 'floral designers' but 'full service' florists who offer the same range of services as a traditional florist shop.

This is not necessarily to say that town centre locations should be avoided in the present day. If the volume of footfall is great enough and the rent and rates reasonable enough then it can still work well.

I would advise anyone considering the purchase of a florist shop to spend a considerable amount of time sitting in your car within sight of the shop. Monitor the number of customers visiting the shop and do this at different times on different days of the week.

Finding the right business for you

When we bought our first shop we were incredibly naïve. My wife Liz had been studying floristry at Hadlow College in Kent and I was still working in I.T. We had both been spending a lot of our free time finding out all we could about how the floristry trade operated. While Liz was primarily looking at the appearance and location of shops for sale I was looking at the financial aspects. I wondered how many of the small shops could possibly cover their costs, let alone make a sensible profit with such low levels of sales.

We eventually found a small shop in a parade next to Crayford railway station in Kent. It was just five miles from our home and seemed to fit the bill. Turnover was modest but it was a clean and tidy little shop that was being run by the owner with part-time help. Examination of the accounts showed a small, but realistic, net profit. After some negotiation our offer was accepted and Liz became the very excited and proud owner of Blooms of Crayford.

When I looked back at this first purchase in later years I frequently searched for lessons we had learnt from it. My main memory is of the day we completed the purchase and the business was handed over to us. It was a Friday and Liz had spent the day in the shop with the previous owner, doing a stock check, finding out where everything was and how things worked.

I arrived at the shop at the end of the day and asked all the questions I could think of. I was concentrating on how all the admin worked and in particular how the Teleflorist relay orders were processed and accounted for. Eventually we shook hands with the previous owner and her husband and they handed over the keys and left.

I can clearly remember Liz and I standing in the shop and looking at each other that Friday evening, realising that at 8.30 the following morning we had to be open for business and that, apart from a Saturday girl, we were on our own.

In retrospect I now think we were very ill prepared, particularly as Liz had never worked in a florist shop – all her experience had been at college. Amazingly and, to be honest, very luckily things went well. Our Saturday girl Monique proved to be a very competent, savvy and likeable girl. Liz proved to be remarkably fast at make-up work and she also took on Miriam and Val, fellow students at Hadlow College, as part-time florists.

I made all the deliveries on that first day in our little Suzuki van and then spent Sunday on admin and setting up a basic accounting system on my computer. I had booked a week's holiday from work and spent it getting to grips with the many facets of a small business operating in an industry that was completely new to me. I returned to work a week later in high spirits. I was convinced that I could see a way out of the I.T. world in to a much simpler and more enjoyable future.

When we decided to look for our second shop, we put a lot of work into finding a good location for a start-up but just could not find one we felt confident about. We then concentrated all our efforts on to finding an established business. We were looking for a relatively large shop, in terms of turnover, and one that was making a reasonable profit. We were also looking for a shop with lots of potential. We wanted to improve and develop a business with a realistic level of investment.

I was still working full time in I.T. and getting very tired of the pressure and the endless need to fly around Europe and the U.S. We started to use every weekend to visit a particular area of the country where there were florist shops for sale. We did research during the week via agents and the Internet and arranged viewing appointments for the weekend.

After a while we began to think we were searching for the impossible. We looked at so many businesses with shaky accounts and this always ruled them out in my view, even if Liz thought the shop had potential. Conversely we also looked at some shops that had good accounts and were being superbly run by dynamic owners. Often this enabled them to command a high price which we felt was too much for us.

If a business is being superbly run you have to consider honestly whether you can maintain the level of success achieved by the current owners. Most of the tired-looking shops had terrible accounts and most of the impressive shops with good books were too expensive.

Some owners decide not to let the staff know when they are putting a business up for sale and are careful not to have the shop advertised in an identifiable way. They arrange viewings outside of shop hours when no staff are around. This is understandable if the owners do not want to unsettle the staff, or if they fear that staff would feel under threat and might start to look for alternative employment. In my experience most staff are usually wary of new owners and take the view of 'better the devil you know'.

We finally found what we were looking for in Cambridge. Biggs and Sons was the longest established florist in Cambridge and occupied large but tired looking premises on the very busy main road leading from Cambridge towards Ely. The shop frontage had very old signage and a rickety old lean-to projecting from above the shop windows. This greatly reduced the natural light in the shop itself. However it was very well situated approximately half way between the city centre and Cambridge Science Park.

Turnover was at a good level but had hardly grown at all over the past three years. This still enabled the business to make a modest but genuine net profit. It had been in the Biggs family since 1923. A combination of advancing years and the lack of another son or daughter who really wanted to manage the shop had convinced the owner that the time had come to hand over to someone else.

The Biggs family had done a great job in building up a large and loyal customer base. They had been one of the very first members of Interflora and there was still memorabilia in the shop relating to the very early days of the organisation.

Before making an offer we revisited the shop at different times of the day. We parked covertly on the opposite side of the road to observe what walk-in trade there was. We were amazed at the number of people who walked in to this very uninviting looking shop and walked out having bought something. This was what finally convinced us to make an offer.

It was so easy to see how, with a relatively modest investment, we could give this shop a completely fresh new image. We realised that we had to do this without alienating the many long-established customers. They kept returning to the shop despite its faded appearance and were clearly happy with both the service and the quality they were receiving.

There are huge advantages to buying an existing business. When a business is already up and running you can concentrate on improving sales and profitability. The business fundamentals will already be in place for staffing, suppliers and equipment and there will be an established client base. Even the slickest new business takes time to build customer goodwill and the level of sales will be slow to increase. If relationships are good (and there is no reason why they shouldn't be) you can benefit from the advice and experience of the previous owners. Crucially the financial history of an existing business can be fully analysed.

Assessing the vendor

As well as checking out the business it is also essential to try to assess the current owners and their reasons for selling. It is important to feel that you really trust the vendors and that what they tell you is verified when you check out the details in the books.

It is also important to find out what other business interests the vendors have. If they are clearly enjoying a good standard of living is this because of the success of the business or do they have other means of income. It is quite possible for someone owning more than one shop to channel sales from other shops in to a poorly performing shop that they would like to dispose of. If they also put some of the stock purchases through their other shops, then it is easy to show a healthy profit in the books of their weakest shop. This makes it possible to sell a poorly performing business for an inflated price. The likelihood is that this business may not even survive as a competitor to their other businesses, especially if the previous owner then targets their old customer base.

Many small floristry businesses are effectively subsidised by the owner's partner having alternative employment. Although Liz made a consistent profit from her first small shop there was no way it could have provided both of us with a living. This is the case with so many small businesses.

At meetings and conferences we met many couples like us where one partner was a florist and the other was in a completely different profession. This partner would typically have good general business skills and could contribute to the floristry business by handling the admin work and often also helping with deliveries.

For a couple to have any real hope of making a living from a small to medium sized floristry business it has to have reached a certain critical mass in terms of the level of sales. I came to the conclusion that no couple can enjoy a good standard of living with an annual turnover of less than at least £250,000 – unless they have some means of acquiring stock at very low cost and/or have unusually low overheads.

Many shops are advertised for sale where just one glance at the essential details of stated turnover, rent, gross profit etc. reveals that the owner cannot be making more than a tiny net profit. However shops like this do still sell – usually to very naïve buyers who have a rose tinted vision of owning their own floristry business. This can often make a florist business much easier to sell than other businesses where potential buyers are focussed more on taking a hard-headed look at the finances.

Adjusting to self-employment

In searching for the right business for you, another important consideration is making the adjustment to being self-employed. If you have been used to regular salaried employment, where you can be reasonably sure of your current and future level of income, then self-employment can be a shock.

When Liz and I first ventured into the floristry world we had both been used to secure salaried income. Making the change to the uncertain world of owning your own business can be a real reality check. Whilst Liz made the change I remained in the I.T. industry for some years until we were confident enough that we could both be sure of a reasonable self-employed income.

I must say that eventually I actually grew to like the uncertainty of owning your own business, but only when we became well established. I liked the challenge of starting the week not really knowing quite what would materialise but being confident in the cash reserves we had behind us.

Over the years many customers told us that they thought it must be lovely to have the opportunity to own a business like ours and work with flowers all day. I often wondered if they would feel the same if they were buying stock inside a refrigerated Dutch lorry at 6am on a cold January morning, or washing the shop floor on a Sunday morning. We understood their enthusiasm though, as we actually wanted to spend lots of time in the shop.

When we first took over the Cambridge shop the staff were very wary of us and wondered what changes we would make. Once they saw us making improvements this quickly changed. We found they were struggling to work with blunt scissors and knives. They sat on stools in the work room that were so old the metal frames were poking through the seat cushions. Things like this we fixed in the very first week. Then we started to modernise the whole shop and improve the wages – this lifted everyone's morale and brought them onside.

If you take over the business and make the mistake of alienating the staff you can quickly find yourself in a nightmarish situation with costs rising, orders going wrong and your investment rapidly diminishing in value. Florists do not take kindly to a new owner criticising their make-up work, especially if they know you can't do a better job yourself.

If the business has a proven track record of rising sales and good profits then this can only be because the staff have been doing a great job. All businesses are a direct reflection of the capabilities of the staff employed. It is possible for a failing business to employ good staff but still fail because of the way it is run. If the business has consistently performed well the staff must be good. Why endanger your investment by taking a heavy-handed approach and letting people know they had better toe the line because you are the boss?

Day-to-day delegation can be difficult for the newly self-employed. When we first took over our Cambridge shop we had days when Liz and I were rushed off our feet, but we were leaving some of the girls without enough to do and this understandably frustrated them.

We seemed to feel that it was unfair if the staff were putting in more hours than us and we didn't want them thinking we were slackers. This was ridiculous because if there are enough staff for the given workload, and the shop is running efficiently, you should feel quite comfortable about taking as much time off as you want. On some relatively quiet days the girls would implore Liz and I to give ourselves a day off. There were times when they literally pushed me out the door and sent me off to the golf course.

The situation is different at peak times like Valentines and Mothers Day when you need every single person working very long hours. Then you need to set an example and work at least as long as any member of staff.

I have to admit I have not always followed my own advice. In our early days I could get very stressed while making deliveries on a busy day and the girls would joke about needing to get their tin hats out. The Cambridge traffic was usually awful and parking in the city centre could be a nightmare. One day, after I had stormed out of the shop in a temper with yet another batch of orders, I returned to find all the girls were literally wearing tin hats! They had on upturned bowls that we used for arrangements. This was a great idea on their part as I then felt completely stupid, we all had a good laugh and I learned a lesson.

The girls often did things like this and on reflection I am grateful they were so patient at times when I must have been difficult to work with. Whenever I was the butt of their jokes it was because I deserved it. I like to think that at least I had the good grace to say sorry and go out to buy them all cream cakes. Mind you, the cakes often got me in to more trouble because of the girl's diets…

Maybe we were lucky in having such great staff but I also like to think we played our part in treating them well, regularly thanking them for their efforts and also we were known as the best paying florist shop in Cambridge.

When Liz took a day off she loved to spend it in the City, shopping and lunching, with her mobile switched off. I liked to spend a morning on the golf course or an afternoon at a football match – again with the mobile switched off. I know many owners who would never dream of turning their phones off in case of some emergency back at the shop.

We always believed in having some strictly private leisure time to ourselves and we knew we could rely on our staff to look after things while we were away. It is important to show your staff that you trust them to make their own decisions when something goes wrong.

Searching for the right business – Checklist

- Can you go it alone?
- Who can handle the business side?
- Leasehold or freehold premises?
- Does the location make sense?
- What can you afford?
- Could you improve it?
- Does it fit with your skills?
- Do you trust the vendor?
- Can you adapt to self-employment?

3 Purchasing an existing business

This chapter addresses:

- Confidentiality agreements
- Examining the accounts
- Financing the purchase
- Using an accountant
- Checking sales and profits
- Checking the costs
- Inspecting the paperwork
- Gross profits and mark-ups
- Claims of unrecorded sales
- Assessing the value
- Making an offer

Confidentiality agreements

Having found a business which appears to fit your needs the next step is to really dig in to the detail. You need to thoroughly analyse all the financial data available. You should ask for the past three year's accounts, including profit and loss statements, balance sheets and all the quarterly VAT returns.

If there is a business transfer agent working on behalf of the seller they will want you to view the business and meet the owners. If they are satisfied that you are a serious prospective purchaser they will usually require you to sign a non-disclosure agreement before they will allow access to any accounting details. This is partly to avoid time-wasters but also to guard against the vendor's competitors gaining valuable inside information.

It is not unknown for a rival to get someone to pose as a prospective purchaser simply to get access to information about sensitive data. This may relate to contract customers, discount arrangements with local funeral directors and all sorts of detail which would be of competitive use to them.

If you are genuinely a seriously interested potential buyer of a business, but still have difficulty getting access to relevant accounting information, then you should be very suspicious as to why this is.

Examining the accounts

Before a large company finalises the purchase of another company it will first carry out the due diligence process. This often involves a small army of accountants verifying the true financial position of the business. They will examine all of the costs and both current and future liabilities. They check the security of the order book and the base of account customers. Every aspect has to be checked to guard against the risk of either over-paying or of buying a business which, had you known the truth, you wouldn't have touched with a barge-pole!

You will not need a small army of accountants but you will almost certainly need the help of an accountant unless you have extensive business experience and the ability to dissect the books of a business. If you are new to the floristry trade you should also seek help and guidance from someone with real experience of actually owning a similar business.

41

My first wife Liz and I were once very interested in buying a florist shop in Florida. We had studied the details of many shops that were for sale and found that the vast majority had shaky accounts, or insufficient turnover, or costs that were out of control. Eventually we drew up a short list of businesses which looked like a feasible purchase, arranged visits to view and made appointments to see agents and vendors.

After a week in Florida we decided the only shop that appeared to tick all our boxes was in Ocala. The shop looked right, the owner seemed like a nice guy and the staff seemed competent and happy. The big problem was the accounts. Getting all the detail I asked for was like pulling teeth.

Eventually between the agent and the vendor they provided us with P&L statements, verified by a certified accountant, covering a period of two years and ending some fifteen months previously. These looked okay but what I really needed were the full details of the last financial year and getting this became a real problem.

We were negotiating just after the financial year-end and the broker claimed, not unreasonably, that he could provide quarterly details but that the accountant had not quite completed the full year-end accounts. He said that we only needed to look at the owner's lifestyle to know that he was making a very good living from the shop. My response was that maybe he had other sources of income – maybe his parents were very wealthy and he was their favourite son!

We returned to the broker's offices the following day and they presented us with detailed quarterly accounts for the first, second and fourth quarters. Bizarrely, the accounts for the third quarter were missing. The broker apologised and said they must be with the accountant but that we shouldn't worry because the missing quarter was very similar to the other quarters.

I explained there was absolutely no way I would make an offer for the business until I had seen the missing quarter. We returned to our hotel having told the broker that unless the Q3 detail was made available by the following day then we would be returning to the UK with no deal.

That evening the broker called me to say that miraculously all the missing paperwork had now been found and it would be available first thing in the morning for us to inspect. I spread-sheeted everything ready to add in the missing quarter and produce my own provisional P&L for the full year-end accounts.

Assuming that everything was in line with what we had been told by the owner and the broker and that we could verify this, Liz and I agreed the details of the offer we would make. We had also been looking at houses in the area, we had the funds in place and provisional visa arrangements made. We were both full of enthusiasm at the prospect of a new life in the U.S.

The next morning we saw the missing Q3 accounts and I knew immediately why they had been so difficult to get hold of. Sales had been very disappointing in that quarter and all sorts of stock costs and exceptional annual costs had been shoehorned in to Q3 to make the other quarters look really good.

I added the missing quarter's figures in to my spreadsheet and produced a rough P&L statement for the full year. The picture of the business was now completely different and the net profit simply wasn't good enough for us to proceed.

When I explained this to the brokers they looked at their feet and were clearly embarrassed. Amazingly, before we left their offices, they asked if I would be interested in working for them as a business broker. I suppose this was some sort of compliment!

This was a clumsy and obvious attempt at deception but it is not uncommon and I have found that many vendors will go to extreme lengths in their attempts to deceive buyers. I have seen people from the U.K. make quite incredible purchases of businesses in both the U.K. and the U.S. People get carried away with a rose-tinted view of what looks like a lovely shop and despite all the warning signs they go ahead regardless.

In my experience almost every vendor will attempt to make their business seem like a more attractive prospect than it really is. Most people will be misleading in some way. They may just omit to tell you certain negative aspects and talk up the positive aspects or they may be downright liars!

The one exception I have come across is the gentleman who sold us our shop in Cambridge. Over the five years we owned that shop I didn't discover anything deceptive at all in what he told us about the business. Every single thing turned out to be true and accurate and we did not experience one nasty surprise. This is very rare indeed but it shows that there are some really honourable vendors out there. Unfortunately in my experience they are just hard to find.

Financing your purchase

Before you even start to look for a business you will obviously have to have some idea of how you will finance the purchase. In addition to the purchase price there are legal costs and all sorts of start-up costs to calculate. You will need sufficient cash reserves to avoid any cash flow problems. Large contract customers may take up to three months to settle an invoice but you will have had to pay for the stock and labour at the time of supplying their products.

Within the first few days of taking over a florist business you will receive invoices for all sorts of essential services, including shop insurance, buildings insurance, vehicle insurance, telephone line rental, card processing services and possibly joining fees for a relay service. There will also be the first demands for rent, rates and water etc. The relay service you opt to join will usually retain some of the monies due to you in the first six months by way of a deposit and they may retain this money for as long as you are a member.

You must start with enough funding to see you through the difficult early days when it will seem that lots of money is going out and far less is coming in.

Your wholesale suppliers may insist on immediate payment to start with. When they get to know you better and confidence is established they will usually allow you to pay on account. I can understand their reluctance as on a number of occasions I have spoken to ashen faced wholesalers who have just discovered that one of their customers who owes them thousands of pounds has gone bust.

I remember one florist business that crashed spectacularly, leaving a trail of unpaid debts. I knew the owner personally and she gave the appearance of being very successful with a beautiful large house and was impressively featured in one of the Sunday supplements. Her wholesalers were happy to let her rack up debt confident that she had the wherewithal to settle eventually. When her business crashed, to everyone's amazement, it became apparent that she owned virtually nothing, including the house.

Few people have enough surplus personal money to be able to afford to go out and buy a business outright. Thanks largely to the property booms of recent decades many people do have enough equity in their house to enable them to fund the acquisition of a business. If you have to borrow the money, then whoever is providing the finance will naturally demand very good security. Typically this will mean that your house will have to be used as collateral.

Check your eligibility for grants, eg. from the government, local authority or any related organisation. Information is available at the government business support help website – www.gov.uk/business-support-helpline

We bought our first florist shop in Kent for cash, but it was only a small shop and we were able to fund it from our personal savings. We would have had to borrow the money to buy a bigger shop. So we concentrated on paying off our mortgage early and building equity for the future.

After several years of hard saving we finally reached a situation where we had paid off the mortgage and sold both the house and the first shop. We then had enough money to buy a house and the business in Cambridge and also to keep some money in reserve as a rainy-day fund for whatever difficulties the future might hold.

So many small business ventures fail in the first three years that lenders are not prepared to take risks on them, unless they have a very convincing business plan. The level of risk will be reflected in the interest rate associated with a loan. Repayments are likely to be a big element of your P&L statements.

My advice is to be very wary of borrowing money from friends or relations, no matter how close you are to them. They may give you a very low rate of interest, but the problems that often follow if the business falls on hard times can be incredibly stressful. Many long-standing friendships have ended in tears because of failed small business ventures.

Instead of borrowing from them, another option is to sell a friend or relation a stake in your business but they must accept the risk involved. If the business prospers this could be an attractive investment for them and, if they have a stake in the business, they are more likely to help you out at peak times. Any investor has to accept that they could potentially lose all of their stake, but they are then much more likely to actively support you to avoid that scenario coming to pass.

Many years ago I stupidly loaned a sum of money to a relative who wanted to buy an antiques business. The business was in very good shape with excellent accounts and was making a healthy level of net profit. He had successfully managed this business for a number of years and consequently I believed he knew the business inside out.

What I didn't know was how inept he would prove to be in comparison with the previous owner. When it came to buying stock and making financial decisions he was absolutely hopeless. The business ultimately failed because of his shortcomings. He wasn't sold a pup and I attached no blame to the previous owner.

This episode taught me that even if you do all the proper groundwork in checking out and purchasing a business it will still fail if it is badly managed. I learned a valuable lesson and vowed never again to loan money to any friend or relative for a business venture.

Using an accountant

Many experienced owners do not use an accountant on a regular basis, except perhaps for the final year-end accounts. They want the sort of bang up-to-date management information that only they can provide themselves. If you employ an accountant it will be some time before you know how the business has performed over a period of time and this can be very inconvenient and sometimes downright dangerous. By the time the accountant finalises the year-end accounts you may find you have problems that should have been addressed many months ago.

I used one of the low-cost commonly available software accounting packages. These products from the likes of Sage are quite simply superb. It takes a little time and work to first set things up but they save you an enormous amount of work and provide you with a wealth of information about your business.

Every Sunday morning I looked at exactly how the business had performed the week before and, how that compared with the same week in the previous year and our average week. I also produced a provisional P&L statement which showed how the business had performed in the 12 month period up to and including that day. With modern software it is incredibly easy to do this – it is just a little data entry and then a few clicks of the mouse.

We played a little game where this weekly information dictated where we ate Sunday lunch. A good net profit for the week saw us eating a very good lunch in one of Cambridge's best restaurants. A smaller profit meant a pub lunch and a loss meant eating at home. Fortunately we rarely ate at home on a Sunday.

Whether or not you already have a good knowledge of business, and the fundamentals of accounting, I would strongly recommend that you still use a qualified accountant. Check through three years of accounts for any business you are considering buying. Bear in mind however that even this level of checking may not be enough.

Most accountants do not have the specialised knowledge of the floristry trade that an experienced owner has. There are potential problems that an accountant may not find. Consequently I would also recommend using any contacts you may have within the floristry sector to study the books with you, whilst still respecting the small print of the non-disclosure agreement you may have signed with an agent or a broker.

So just what are you looking for when you study the accounts? Essentially you are seeking the truth! Firstly you want to know the sales turnover and the real net profit. If these are poor you may not wish to proceed any further unless the asking price is low and you have a realistic plan for improvement.

Level of sales and profits

Earlier in this book I said that to make a real living from a florist business then the annual sales should be at least £250,000.

However, for many people, the business is not their sole source of income and many people can and do manage on a smaller turnover.

When we bought our first shop in 1995 the previous year's sales had been just £50,000. Because we considered it our first step in a long-term plan, and because I had a well-paid job in I.T., this little shop fully met our objectives. After four years turnover had grown by 80% and the net profit was 10%. Thus the net profit was a measly £9,000 but we then sold the shop for 40% more than we had paid for it.

Much more importantly though we had both learnt an enormous amount and were ready to move on and buy a much larger shop from which we could both make a living. For me it was also an escape route out of the stressful world of I.T. management into a new and very different industry.

It is a considerable risk to buy a large shop as your first venture, even if you have the financial means to do so. It would be essential for the shop to have excellent staff, including a manager capable of taking full responsibility for the day-to-day running of the business. As a new, inexperienced owner you could learn the business from the staff, however the staff would have to be very competent and totally trustworthy.

They would not take kindly to a new and inexperienced owner commenting on the quality of their work and suggesting changes, until the owner could demonstrate that they could do it better.

The P&L statement will give you the figures for sales, stock costs, general operating expenses and the net profit. You have to dig much deeper to analyse the numbers and work out exactly what you could really expect to make from that business.

Checking the costs

One of the most obvious things to check is the real cost of labour. This may be very different from the figure shown in the wages line of the P&L statement. If the owners are actively working in the business you need to find out how they are remunerated.

They may pay themselves wages in the same way they pay the staff, which will give an accurate reflection of the number of hours they work and a realistic hourly rate of pay. If this is included in the totals for the wages costs then all well and good. However, many owners prefer not to pay themselves a regular wage. They take money from the business as and when they need it. This is referred to as drawings on the business' accounts and may not show up in the accounting information provided.

You must try to establish how many hours a week the proprietors typically put in and then estimate a fair hourly rate for the work they do. This figure should then be added to the general wages costs to produce a more accurate representation of the total labour costs. Only then can you examine what impact this has on the true net profit.

For example, the P&L statement of a shop might show a net profit of £50,000. You discover that the two owners of the business are both working in the shop full time. Their roles might typically earn each of them a total of perhaps £20,000 and thus the real net profit is reduced to just £10,000.

Many purchasers don't make the necessary checks on wage costs and can end up in a situation where they have effectively just bought themselves a job, rather than a truly profitable business. You should ask for detailed information about each person employed, their hourly wage and the number of hours worked per week. Also take account of what overtime was worked at peak times and find out what rate this was paid at.

Calculate the true total cost of labour, including the employer's National Insurance contributions and pension contributions and then compare the total with the figures in the P&L statement.

Vendors and agents will often quote a figure for 'add backs'. These are costs that the owners choose to put through the books, often for tax reasons, but which they believe a new owner should not perceive to be real costs. They might include private motoring, home computing, personal stationery and postage, cleaning materials, refreshments, home utility bills, private telephone costs and a host of other things.

As an example, the owner might spend an average of two days a week at home working on shop administration. It is only fair that a proportion of the household bills for heat, light and rates etc. should appear in the shop accounts.

What is much more dubious is when figures for depreciation of capital items, such as delivery vehicles, appear in the P&L statement classed as amounts that should be added back into the net profit. Depreciation of vehicles is a real cost and should be considered as part of the true costs of the business. Even though the vehicles may already be bought and paid for, a business should always be making provision for their reducing value and the need to replace them in the future.

Inspecting the paperwork

To verify the figures shown in the accounts ask for copies of the VAT returns to satisfy yourself that they correspond. Also ask to see copies of bank statements, debtor and creditor lists and supplier's invoices. You must satisfy yourself that all these correspond with what is in the accounts.

Owners must keep detailed records for a period of at least six financial years to comply with tax regulations. This is because they may be subject to an inspection by HMRC at any time. Much of our loft space has been taken up with boxes of paperwork relating to the financial affairs of different businesses.

They proved invaluable some years ago when we had a VAT inspection. Two officials from HMRC spent the best part of a day in my office randomly checking paperwork. They were very appreciative that everything was correctly filed and that I could quickly find everything they asked for. I suspect that the tone of the visit would have been much less friendly if I had spent ages scrabbling through piles of unsorted invoices.

They examined sales records and supplier invoices and all the statements from the supplier of our relay service. The outcome of the visit was a demand for a small payment but I was so convinced everything was in order that I appealed and then this demand was subsequently waived.

I have been almost disappointed that each time we put a shop up for sale no prospective purchaser has ever asked to check the veracity of our records. I have always kept the sort of detailed records that I would expect any buyer to want to see. I would have been pleased to prove that all the paperwork did exist and was correct. Not only would it have proved the accuracy of the figures in the accounts but it would also have made all the effort seem worthwhile!

It is particularly important to check that the figures relating to relay transactions have been correctly applied to the accounts. I have been a member of both Interflora and Teleflorist and both supplied detailed invoices, statements and accounting guidelines.

Interflora provided very detailed guidance in a Finance Handbook that they issued to all their members. If the instructions are not correctly followed then it is quite possible for the accounts of the business to be completely distorted. You may not know this if you take over a business and continue to use the same accounting methods as the previous owner and you could receive a terrible shock when the VAT inspector pays a visit. I have known a chartered accountant get the relay finances completely wrong with regard to how the transactions should be treated for VAT purposes so beware.

Gross profits and mark-ups

The gross profit figure also needs close examination to get a picture of what sort of mark-up the owners have been applying and what sort of stock wastage was the norm. The mark-up on the wholesale purchase of stock typically applied by shop owners is a multiplier of at least 2.5 and ideally up to 3.0.

We should take a moment here to examine what exactly is meant by gross profit in a florist business. Most retail businesses buy goods from wholesalers in a condition ready to be resold to customers. For example a shoe shop buys shoes and doesn't do anything to them except sell them to customers. Thus the gross profit (or gross margin) is simply the difference between what the goods are bought for and what they are sold for.

Gross profit to a car manufacturer is quite different because as well as buying (or manufacturing) all the component parts of a car these then have to be assembled to make the end product. To calculate their gross profit they take the cost of all the parts AND the cost of all the employees who work on the assembly line and then deduct the total from their sales. They do not count all their other operating expenses or the salaries of all their other staff not directly involved in the actual assembly work, eg. managers, designers, marketing staff, HR, security etc.

A florist shop is different again because some of the goods bought in are simply resold (cut flowers, vases etc.) whereas some of the goods are made in to various bouquets and arrangements. Therefore strictly speaking a florist should divide their wages costs between what relates to "manufacture" and what relates to simply serving a customer.

In practice very few florist shops do this – they simply deduct the cost of goods from the total sales to arrive at their gross profit. The only exception I have seen is in a few large shops where some staff only serve customers and others only work on make-up. Then it becomes easy to calculate a real gross profit. In most shops there are typically only a few staff and everyone does everything – serving a customer one minute and making a hand-tied the next.

So we will assume that every business is using the simplified 'sales minus purchases' approach to describe their gross profit.

Many florists will take the price per stem, net of VAT, that they pay the wholesaler. This is then trebled to arrive at a retail price that includes VAT. If you calculate the VAT implications this works out to be a real multiplier of 2.5. I believe this should be the absolute minimum to aim for and you should actually seek to improve on this without becoming known for higher prices than those charged by your direct competitors.

Take an example of a stem bought from a wholesaler for £1 plus VAT. This would typically be sold in a shop for £3 including VAT. You can reclaim the 20p VAT which you paid to the wholesaler. The 50p VAT that your customer pays belongs to HMRC. After the VAT calculations you are left with a real margin of £1.50. Believe me it is very tough to make a reasonable net profit if your margin is less than this and you should really be aiming higher.

This does not mean that the gross sales should necessarily work out at 2.5 times the cost of stock because account has to be taken of wastage. Other items such as sundries, giftware etc. have different multipliers applied to them. After stripping out the VAT, and adjusting for the lower margins typically achieved on relay orders, it is more realistic for the total sales to be approximately double the total purchases. This represents a gross profit margin of 50 per cent.

In my experience it is always best to aim for a higher GP than this – as much as 60 per cent - to actually achieve a realistic GP of circa 50 per cent after wastage and unforeseen problems have been accounted for. Wastage will typically write off around 3 per cent of the purchased stock and often, if stock rotation is not managed carefully enough, this figure can be considerably higher.

A typical and realistic situation is a gross profit of between 45 to 55 percent. This is arrived at by deducting the total cost of all purchases from the total sales and then dividing the result by the total sales. Once all other costs for wages and general operating expenses etc. have been deducted you arrive at a net profit. Probably the average net profit margin across the floristry industry is circa 10 percent.

As an example, this means that a business with total sales of £300,000 will be spending a total of some £150,000 on stock, £120,000 on wages and all other operating expenses, leaving a true net profit of £30,000. Some businesses will do better than this and some will do worse.

Size really does matter when it comes to sales turnover. The bigger the business the smaller all of the non-stock costs should be as a percentage of sales and thus the net profit should improve.

With a smaller business the converse is true and net profit may fall well below 10 percent. The key thing is to achieve a certain critical mass whereby key costs such as wages and rent become a smaller than average percentage of the total sales.

The claimed gross profit of a business can vary enormously. I see florist shops for sale where the owners are claiming anything between 40 and 65 percent gross profit and sometimes even more. Claims at the higher end should be taken with a very large pinch of salt. I have usually found that a close inspection of their accounts will show their claims are unjustified.

A shop in a prime town centre location may have a high gross profit because they can charge premium prices. However, their rent and business rates are likely to be much higher than average and so their high operating expenses will reduce the net profit significantly.

You need to ask questions about just what mark-up has been used and why. If the mark-up has been low it may give new owners the opportunity to raise prices. This could increase the profit per sale but may reduce the volume of sales.

The owners may have been forced to use low mark-ups because of fierce local competition. However, there are some shops which under-price because of sheer naivety. If the mark-up has been higher than average this may be because the customer base is relatively affluent and products are not particularly price sensitive. A florist shop in central London will typically have to apply high mark-ups to compensate for their very high costs for rent, rates and labour etc.

Claims of high gross profit margins can be very misleading and in assessing a business you should focus more on the true net profit that has actually been achieved.

Claims of unrecorded sales

One aspect that is difficult and usually impossible to ascertain is the thorny issue of sales that don't go through the books. Many vendors will claim that lots of cash sales are not rung up on the till. This can never be verified.

A decision on whether or not to make an offer for a business should always be based on the verifiable accounts of the business although an assessment of what the vendor tells you is always likely to have some impact.

If a customer in a hurry slaps £60 on the counter to pay for his hand-tied bouquet and dashes straight out of the shop to avoid getting a parking ticket this leaves the owner with a choice to make. If he rings up the sale on the till then £10 of that £60 will go in VAT and ultimately another £14 on the owner's tax and N.I. contributions leaving a net amount of £36.

Thus the owner has to decide whether to be totally honest and make £36 from this sale or whether to be opportunistic and pocket the full £60.

I am not suggesting an owner should break the law but it would be naïve in the extreme to assume that every shop owner is scrupulously honest and always puts absolutely everything through the books.

HMRC inspectors are aware of what is the norm for each and every type of business. Most owners know that tax inspectors have guidelines of what to expect and what to look out for. In terms of sales in relation to costs they will know if an owner is being unreasonably greedy. Some owners will stop bending the rules once they decide to put a business up for sale.

They may tell you that they have been taking lots of money that doesn't go through the till, whereas they might actually have been ringing everything up to make the books look better. The safe thing is to believe only the numbers relating to sales which have been processed correctly.

After taking over a business you may get a pleasant surprise if the staff confide to you that the previous owners were indeed pocketing a lot of cash. Whether or not you decide to continue this practise is up to you but you have to understand that should you get caught by HMRC the penalties are very severe.

Assessing the value of a business

I cannot repeat too often that you really must do your homework. Assess the worth of a business by what you observe and can verify for yourself in the accounts.

When buying a house it is standard practice to have a solicitor make the appropriate searches. They check for any external factors that may affect the value of the asset in the future. The same concerns apply when buying a business. If there are plans to build a by-pass, which may greatly reduce your passing trade, this would be a big worry. On the other hand, plans to build a big new housing estate nearby might considerably increase your customer base in the future.

Let's assume that you have done all your homework as diligently as possible. You have looked at the business, the stock and the accounts. You have studied the business trends, the customer base, the competition and all the possible threats and opportunities. You have also assessed the current owners and the staff as best you can. Now you have to decide what sort of offer you might make. Before you can do this you obviously have to think long and hard about what the business is worth to you.

You will need access to sufficient funds to buy the goodwill, the stock, fixtures and fittings and vehicles. You will also need enough for the start-up costs and solicitor's fees, plus sufficient reserves to ensure you have no cash flow problems in the first few months.

A proportion of the asking price will be for fixtures and fittings and these should be detailed separately. You should check all these assets to see if the amount asked truly represents their actual worth.

The value of the stock is usually jointly agreed by both the vendor and the purchaser. This is normally accomplished by doing a stock check at the time of completing the sale. This valuation should be based on the wholesale cost of all the stock that is deemed to be of good merchantable quality. You should not pay for stock that is clearly old and grubby. If you don't think that you could sell any particular item then don't pay for it.

The value of motor vehicles is also usually kept separate from other assets. This is best verified by personally checking the condition and mileage and studying the guide price for the model of van or car. This is easy to do on one of the motor vehicle valuation websites such as Glass's Guide at www.glass.co.uk or alternatively at What Van magazine at www.whatvan.co.uk

In assessing the value of trade vehicles some allowance should be made for any signwriting, as impressive graphics will add value but any shoddy amateurish signage will lower it. Ask for verification of what the owner paid for the signage and assess it's condition. For example , assume the owner bought a van for £10,000 and the guide price is now £5,000. If the owner paid £500 for good quality signage, and this is still in pristine condition, then it would be reasonable to value it at £250.

By far the biggest asset of the typical florist shop is the goodwill and the asking price will consist mostly of this. It is a reflection of the volume of sales that have been built up over the lifetime of the business by virtue of the efforts and the investment made by the owners. This may be related to an earnings multiple or the return on capital employed. The earnings multiple is typically between two and three times what you have assessed the true net profit to be. This is after making adjustments to the net profit declared in the accounts for such things as genuine add-backs and owner's wages etc.

As an example, the value of goodwill for a shop that you assess to be making a true net profit of £20,000 per annum is assessed at between £40,000 and £60,000. Whether it is at the upper or lower end of that scale will depend upon the trends shown in the past three year's accounts and the potential for future growth.

For a business that can demonstrate consistent growth in sales, in an improving location, the multiple will be at the high end. A business that has experienced flat, or even declining, sales or which is located in an area experiencing hard times, will merit a low valuation and may represent an unacceptable risk at any price.

You might prefer to value a business based upon the return on capital invested. To do this you must work out the rate of return you want from whatever capital you have to invest. This will obviously be a much higher rate than if you simply invested your money in a bank or building society because the risk is higher and the returns much less certain.

Typically a buyer of a florist shop would be looking for a return of some 20 per cent on the capital invested, before interest and tax. If you estimate that the grand total you need to invest is £100,000 then you should feel confident about making an annual net profit of circa £20,000 to justify this.

Part of your assessment will depend on how competent an owner you honestly believe you will be in comparison with the present owner. Is the current owner a talented dynamic type who is moving on to bigger things or are they tired and unenthusiastic and looking forward to retirement?

Of course, the real worth of any business is what someone is prepared to pay for it. Any valuation methods similar to those described will go out of the window if a purchaser wants the business badly enough.

I have known many people in the floristry sector to buy a particular business primarily because what they are really doing is buying into a new way of life. Even though the asking price may be high, the financial returns low, and the hours long and hard, many people are just so enthusiastic about the prospect that they are prepared to pay far more than a hard-headed businessperson would.

I can only repeat that you must beware of the rose-tinted view of playing with flowers all day. Floristry is hard work and it is a tough way to make a living.

Making an offer

Having worked out what you believe is the true worth of the business you should set an upper limit on what you are prepared to pay and then assess what your opening offer should be. If you genuinely believe the shop has been undervalued, and there are lots of people interested, then a low offer might mean you run the risk of missing the boat. Do not allow yourself to get carried away by what the agent and the vendor tell you about the level of interest but try to verify it. How long has the business been on the market and why are the owners selling?

An offer that is ridiculously low can alienate the vendor and may cause problems at a later stage. If the vendor reluctantly accepts a low offer they may want to strike a much harder bargain when you come to agree a valuation for stock and vehicles etc. It is always best to conduct negotiations in such a way that an amicable on-going relationship is forged with the vendor. They can be an enormous help with the many questions you will have once you have taken over. These questions may relate to customer requirements, regular annual orders, invoicing of account customers and historical information on peak periods. Maintaining good relations will help you enormously in the future.

While some businesses sell at the full asking price there are some that eventually sell for less than half of the original price. I have looked at shops in poor locations, with terrible accounts and no discernible potential. Having dismissed them as 'unsaleable' I have subsequently been staggered to discover that they sold for close to the asking price.

From talking to other owners over the years I would estimate that the average price typically achieved by florist businesses up for sale is around 80 per cent of the original asking price, although I have no hard evidence of this. An initial offer could be as low as 75 per cent of the asking price. This clearly depends on what you believe to be the true worth of the business, the level of interest from other prospective purchasers and how desirable the business is to you personally.

If prospective purchasers are queuing up for viewings, and the vendor has a genuine reason for a quick sale, then a higher offer might be justified. You want to avoid missing out on a really good opportunity but you must resist being carried away by misplaced optimism. Estate agents just love viewers who fall madly in love with a house and cannot disguise this. They quickly offer the full asking price and it is accepted. Often the agent returns to their office chuckling at their naivety. Be sure you don't make this same mistake.

When we bought the shop in Cambridge the asking price was reasonable but there were many other factors that influenced us to make an offer. The shop had enormous potential and we were very impressed by the staff. The books were good, access was easy and there was plenty of parking. We felt absolutely certain that we could rapidly increase sales and profitability and this proved to be the case.

We sold this business only because of my wife's terminal illness. With good verifiable accounts and solid growth we had prospective buyers competing with each other. A quick sale for the full asking price was easy to achieve and I could almost certainly have achieved a higher sale figure by letting prospective purchasers get in to a bidding war. However, the main motivation was to sell quickly and in the event the day of completing the sale turned out to be just three days before Liz passed away.

Having agreed a price the agent will want a deposit of up to 10 per cent to show your commitment to proceeding with the purchase. Solicitors acting for each party will then need to finalise the contract of sale. They will handle all the necessary legal work relating to the leasehold or freehold.

Whether you take out a new lease, or have the balance of an existing lease assigned to you, will affect the length of time the whole transaction will take. An assignment of an existing lease is usually much quicker to arrange. You will have to assess the benefits of this against the reduced security of tenure in the future.

I really cannot stress enough that the key thing is to do your homework as thoroughly as possible. Once you have signed on the dotted line and the sale is completed there is no turning back so be safe and not sorry.

Buying an existing business – checklist

- Take advice from an experienced florist
- Check out three year's accounts
- Use an accountant
- Calculate all the start-up costs
- Check the wages, do the owners pay themselves?
- Check all the VAT returns, do they correspond?
- Are the claimed add-backs legitimate?
- Be wary of unrecorded sales claims
- Use a solicitor to check the lease
- Don't pay for unsaleable stock
- Make sure you have enough cash reserves
- Assess the value of the goodwill element
- Maintain good relations
- Don't overpay
- Keep a cool head!

4 Starting a New Business

This chapter addresses:

- Deciding how to start
- Working from home
- Getting set up
- Sales and marketing
- Developing a website
- Building a customer base
- Moving on to 'Floral Designer

Deciding how to start

Let's now assume that you have looked at the idea of purchasing an existing business but have ruled this out. Maybe you are worried about the cost or perhaps the uncertain future of the traditional florist shop.

For whatever reason, you have come to the conclusion that you want to start your own business. This could be a shop or you may prefer a more cautious approach that enables you to settle into the world of retail floristry and build gradually. Your decision will rest partly on your own personal circumstances.

You may feel that you wish to quickly develop a business which can provide you with a living. This will entail a lot of drive, very long hours and absolute commitment. It certainly isn't something you could do on a part-time basis unless you plan to employ somebody to run the business for you while you concentrate on whatever is your primary occupation.

You may be looking for something much less ambitious to start with. Maybe you are already quite busy with your home and your children but feel that you would like to develop a love of flower arranging into something which could provide you with some pocket money.

The 'home florist' route has been a good entry point for many people who have taken advantage of increased free time as the children grow up and become more independent.

You can only really aspire to be an up-market Floral Designer once you have a lot of experience of handling weddings, regular contract work, funerals and events. To make this leap you must invest a significant amount into building a superb website, which gives the impression that you are probably operating from fancy premises in a prime location in a well-heeled town or city.

In practice you may still be working from home if you have plenty of space, or from a cheap lock-up unit. It doesn't really matter too much as most of your customers will want you to come to them.

The option of starting a mail order floristry business, again requires a lot of investment in sales and marketing and a superb website. The main difference is the reduced skill level required for this type of operation. You don't have to be a highly skilled and experienced florist to box up cut flowers and basic bouquets and send them out by post.

Most of the businesses operating in this sector will have a very limited range of products. Over recent years the materials used for packaging have improved significantly, but many of the products require some work on the part of the recipient to arrange the flowers attractively. Mostly you need a good grasp of the commercial logistics involved in mail-order.

Working from home

So let's assume you have worked hard and gained some floristry qualifications and got some experience, perhaps by working in a florist shop. This isn't necessarily essential as I have known people set themselves up as a home florist with their only real experience being gained at college.

The key question is really whether you believe you are good enough. If someone phoned you up to order a hand-tied bouquet, or a funeral spray, or a pedestal arrangement, could you do it? Do you have sufficient confidence in your own ability to get paid a sensible price for what you could produce? Do you feel that the customer will be just as pleased with your products as they would be if they had bought them in a florist shop?

Probably you have already acquired the basic tools of the floristry trade whilst doing a college course but you will need to build on this to be able to handle a wide range of work.

Maybe you know an experienced florist who you could call for advice when you receive your first big order, and you start to panic about how to acquire the right stock and be able to deliver on time.

Most home florists start gradually by doing work for family and friends and then getting other work by word of mouth. Probably the most important thing is to charge sensible commercial prices from the very beginning. Many home florists initially don't charge much as they do bits and pieces of work for brothers, sisters, aunts, uncles and friends.

After a while the home florist realises that although these friendly customers are very pleased with what is produced for them, they aren't actually making any money from this time-consuming work. To then start charging these same friendly customers a price that is closer to typical commercial prices comes as a shock to them and they might wonder if they are being taken advantage of.

I believe it is best to start as you mean to go on. You can afford to undercut the local florist, as you don't have all the overheads they have, but charge perhaps 80 per cent of what the florist shop would charge and not 50 per cent. You won't have to add VAT to the price but you won't be able to reclaim the VAT you paid when buying the stock from the wholesaler.

Getting set up

Before you start think very carefully about where you are going to work. The kitchen table might be fine to start with but getting all your tools, oasis, wire and various sundries out after the family has finished breakfast and clearing it all away before lunch will soon become a real pain.

If you have an out-building, which you can convert into a workshop, that could be ideal, but again you need to think carefully. It needs to be insulated, with plenty of power points and storage for all your sundries and equipment. The key element is the work surface. A large table is ideal but the ideal solution is a workbench on wheels at the correct height to enable you to avoid back problems.

Having a mobile workbench enables you to work on large pieces of work with plenty of space for turning the item as you work. A two metre double ended coffin spray takes up a lot of space. Optimise the workbench by adding shelving and drawers underneath so you can have all your essential equipment and accessories close to hand.

You will need good lighting and some form of heating to avoid damp. Think about how you could add more workspace when you unexpectedly get two large orders in the same week and need to rope in another florist to help you.

If you suddenly find yourself with more work than you have the space for, you will need some sort of contingency plan. Perhaps you have a friend or relative with space you could use temporarily. Maybe somebody would be prepared to loan you their garage for a few days.

If you have a good size garden, think about what sources of foliage you have and what flowers you could grow. A good size laurel hedge can save a home florist a lot of money over the years. British flowers are popular again now with many people wanting to support the use of locally sourced produce, so find out who is growing what in your area.

Check out your local wholesalers – compare their ranges of stock, pricing and whether they are prepared to offer you any discount if you become a regular customer.

Make sure you register as self-employed with HMRC. You must declare your earnings from your floristry work but you can offset the cost of all your stock, sundries, equipment, insurance, car use, heat and light etc. against this.

Incidentally insurance is essential as you must have protection against claims from customers that something you have done or provided caused them some form of illness or injury. If a customer had an allergic reaction to a flower you used, then in today's litigious world they might sue.

Sales and marketing

Having your own website is absolutely essential if you are serious about making money from any sort of retail floristry activity. Don't think you will get enough business from having lots of local contacts, word of mouth and local advertising. We now live in a world where no business is considered to be a serious player if they have no presence on the internet.

Unless you have very good I.T. skills and are an exceptionally talented photographer, with real artistic flair, don't even think about cobbling together your own website. Use a professional website design service – these aren't particularly expensive and there are sure to be plenty of people offering this sort of service in your area. Seek recommendations and check out work they have done by visiting relevant websites.

Get some professional business cards and produce a leaflet showing your range of products and services. Highlight your website address and phone numbers and if you are reasonably photogenic include a photo of yourself so people can see who they will be dealing with. A thousand attractive colour leaflets can cost as little as a hundred pounds.

Personally I have always been disappointed with the results of advertising in local newspapers and magazines and from talking to other florist shop owners it is apparent that most of them hold a similar view. The only exception I have found is to write an 'advertorial' about your business. This is an article about your business in which you can showcase what you do and how well you do it and most of the print media will print it if you also pay for an advert to appear alongside it.

I have typically found that most of the print media is short of copy and they welcome an opportunity to fill a page, whilst also boosting their advertising revenue.

Put a lot of effort into distributing your cards and leaflets. Take them to local galleries, hairdressers, cafes and hotels etc. Take advantage of community noticeboards in shops, supermarkets, post offices, tourist information offices, town halls etc.

Offer local hotels and businesses an attractive deal for supplying them with flowers on a regular basis. Try to establish friendly relations with receptionists in all sorts of local businesses. Even if they don't want reception flowers on a regular basis they will

69

probably be asked by the company's employees if they can recommend a local florist.

When a new business set up an office in Cambridge we would supply them with a complimentary arrangement for the reception desk. Often this turned into a regular contract and we gained lots of spin-off business from the workforce. For our best spending contract customers we always supplied a Xmas bouquet and a diary for the receptionist. Receptionists are very important contacts to have so when you get to know one look after them!

Developing a website

Don't think that because you are 'only' a home florist then you won't need a presence on the internet. Maybe you can't afford the cost of using a professional website designer but for very little money you can at least create your own basic website and get a foothold in the world of E-commerce. There are on-line services which enable almost anyone with a little knowledge of home computing to use a template and develop their own website. It may be basic but it can still be attractive and functional and it will show people that you belong to today's world.

You may not want customers to be able to buy on-line from you at this stage but you do need to let people know where you are and what you offer. You may want to simply let people know what area you cover rather than giving your home address, particularly if you are operating from a house in a residential road.

If you are competent enough to offer a similar range of products to the typical florist shop it is easy to actually give the impression that you are a shop and many people do this. So long as you are not telling any lies and are simply giving the impression that you are a 'full service florist' then there is nothing wrong with this.

Many customers will not care about the premises you operate from so long as they can buy their attractive and well-made bouquet or arrangement at a competitive price.

Using Google to do a brief search of the internet will show you how many people are taking advantage of using the internet to create an impression of a successful established business. You don't have to make it too obvious just what is behind the gloss! So make the most of what you can offer but do it in a way that is both honest and legal.

Include good quality well shot photographs of all the stock items that you offer. Stress that you also specialise in weddings, funerals, corporate events and contract work for business customers. Include some testimonials from previous customers.

One of the key reasons businesses are so keen to build their online sales is because of the greatly reduced cost of sale for each online transaction. In the typical florist shop it is relatively costly to have somebody spending time talking to a customer to determine their requirements, take all their details down on to an order form and process a card transaction.

Businesses just love online sales. They get the opportunity to show customers all the options, encourage them to add on extras and make suggestions along the lines of 'customers who bought x frequently also bought y'. The customer keys in all their details relating to addresses, messages and card numbers. All this automation greatly reduces the staffing costs whilst increasing the average spend per sale. The difference in profitability is enormous.

In later chapters of this book we will cover optimising your website to make it as easy as possible for potential customers to find you. Search engine optimisation has become almost a science in itself and understanding this means a whole world of difference in today's online marketplace.

Also we will look at how you can harness social media to help build your customer base and keep them informed of all the new and interesting products and services you can offer.

Building a customer base

Whilst every business is always seeking new ways to find new customers it is also very important to look after the ones you already have. It is a well-known maxim in business that the easiest customers to sell to are the ones you already have, your existing customer base.

In today's world many large businesses in the utility and insurance sectors offer all their best deals only to new customers, which infuriates many of their loyal customers who have been with them for years. I assume that when they analyse their financials they must know that this is the way to maximise profitability, but it certainly doesn't give their customers a warm feeling.

I have always believed in looking after your existing customers and offering them incentives to stay with you. Loyalty cards certainly seem to work for the supermarkets, although these types of schemes are expensive to administer.

For the typical florist the easiest way to keep in touch with your customers is via social media and particularly by having an online blog (also called a weblog). This can be part of your website and is like an online diary written in an informal style and regularly updated.

If you start a blog it is absolutely key to maintain it and keep thinking of topical and seasonal things to write about. If you forget about it for a month, regular visitors will quickly get bored and come to the conclusion that you are not very serious about it.

I always found that giving away a diary to our best spending 100 customers was a good investment. A nice diary with your shop name, phone number and website details costs only a few pounds. I liked to give them to customers around October time which improved our chances of them starting to use it before they were given more diaries. An alternative but similar idea is a calendar. Either way it is a low-cost method of having your name and contact details in prominent view right through the year.

As an Interflora member I also took advantage of their gold card scheme. These cards looked up-market and carried the shop name, phone number and website address in addition to the Interflora logo. When a customer got out their wallet or purse in the shop we frequently noticed one of our cards and we became convinced it was another inexpensive way to keep us in the customer's mind.

Some businesses offer a discount to gold card holders but this can be fraught with difficulty as it is not a good idea to give a discount across the board on all your products. In the current marketplace florists make such tiny margins on relay orders that any discount can turn this into a loss.

Also bear in mind that sales discounts must massively increase your order volumes if they are to make any financial sense. We will address this subject in more detail later, in the chapter on sales.

In the floristry sector I have typically found that either the customer will go for an item or they won't. A bit of discount won't make much difference except to your profits. I don't really have any proof of this - it is simply my own personal view based on my experience.

Moving on to Designer Florist

If you have been successful in building your business as a home florist you will probably reach a stage when you wonder if you could step up to the Floral Designer role.

Perhaps you have successfully provided the flowers for some large weddings and also handled some corporate events. Customers perceive your work to be of the very highest quality and you have gained lots of spin-off customers who have heard about work you have done. You have been to demos given by well-known designers and you honestly believe that your talent and skills are on a par with theirs.

Your sales have risen steadily but you have become frustrated that the level of business you get doesn't provide you with an income you could live on. Even if you believe you have the potential to aim higher you must consider your potential customer base very carefully.

You will need to be operating in an area with a lot of potential contract customers and general affluence. The typical customers of a Floral Designer are well-heeled people who are prepared to spend big to get the desired results for weddings, parties, funerals and all manner of special events.

Floral designers in the London area can earn hundreds of pounds just for one dinner party for a handful of guests. A larger party in a residential house can see the bill rise in to the thousands. Some customers have a regular weekly contract for the supply and arrangement of flowers around the house, which again can run into hundreds of pounds.

You also need a good base of professional office premises, hotels, restaurants and bars. Regular weekly contracts are worth their weight in gold and invariably lead to all sorts of spin-off business.

One company in Cambridge wanted regular weekly flowers for their reception area. They then asked us to provide large planted troughs full of plants which we had to maintain for them. A gift-wrapped bouquet was delivered to each of their employees on their birthday and each year on St. Georges Day they wanted a red rose delivered to each and every employee.

Over the years several of their employees then used us for their weddings, for wive's birthdays, anniversaries and funerals. The total spend relating to that one company over a five year period was many thousands of pounds and I still swap Christmas cards with their receptionist today.

As a Designer Florist this is the type of customer you need and if you look after them properly the dividends can be enormous.

Typically there are two big investments you need to make to move up into this role – E-commerce and space. The Ecommerce part of it needs tackling right away but the acquisition of more space to work in can be gradual.

You most certainly need a beautiful professionally designed and produced website with lots of stunning photographs. Not the sort of website mentioned earlier for the typical home florist but something much more impressive and extensive.

A lot of florists try to handle the photography themselves to save money but in my experience unless you are a superbly talented photographer this doesn't work. If you browse the net you can easily spot the home-made websites from the truly professional up-market ones.

It might need an investment of perhaps five thousand pounds to get a good enough website and you might think you will need to gain an awful lot of lucrative orders to get your money back, but this is the sort of investment you need to make if you are really serious about this.

With regard to space this depends very much on your own circumstances. If you can use your own garage and an outbuilding then you may already have the solution. Some people rent a lock-up unit on an industrial estate and some have a suitable sized large shed-type building erected in their garden.

Make it generally known to your friends and neighbours that you need to rent some work space somewhere convenient and who knows what suggestions they might come up with. You may find somebody you know has a large outbuilding which you could use – they could get some welcome income from your rent and this is likely to be an awful lot cheaper than renting a lock-up.

The caveat is that you must ensure you have the appropriate permission to be using the building on a regular basis for business purposes. The neighbours might get upset if they start to regularly see large wholesaler's lorries clogging up the road. Don't get yourself into hot water with the local authority if a neighbour complains.

Think about how you will cope if you are presented with the opportunity to provide all the flowers for a big corporate event in the same week as a large wedding. You may need to make a number of large pedestal arrangements, bouquets, corsages and have to decorate a hall, a church, a marquee and a hotel banqueting room. If you turn away this type of work you can get a reputation of not being able to handle large events. It is better to build a network of home florists and part-timers who you can employ as and when you need to.

Starting a new business – checklist

- How much time can you give?
- What space can you use?
- What investment can you make?
- Do you understand the mail-order sector?
- Have a clear sales and marketing strategy
- Can you develop a website?
- How will you develop a customer base?
- Can you move up to Floral Designer?
- Do you have enough ambition to make the investment in both time and money?

ב Sales and Marketing

This chapter addresses:

-   The easy way to improve your profits
-   Advertising
-   Telesales
-   Distance selling regulations
-   Sales in a shop
-   Flower subscriptions
-   Keeping tabs on competitors
-   Business hours
-   Customer confidentiality
-   Networking
-   Weddings
-   Funerals
-   Signage and layout
-   Dealing with your competitors

The easy way to increase your profits

Marjorie and Pippa work in two competing florist shops in a small town. Dave and Steve are both men who have new ladies in their lives who they both want to please and impress.

Dave walks in to shop A and is met by a smiling Marjorie. He doesn't know much about flowers and is a little nervous about showing his ignorance. He met Samantha only two months ago but has already fallen deeply in love with her. He wants to buy her something which will hopefully show her just how much he cares for her.

'How much is a bouquet?' Dave asks nervously.

'Bouquets start at £20' says Marjorie.

'OK I'll have one of those please' replies Dave, thankful that he hasn't displayed his ignorance.

Marjorie quickly makes up a very basic gift wrap, using mostly carnations and chrysants. Dave pays, picks out a card, writes it, thanks her and goes out feeling thankful that is over.

After the cost of stock, cello and ribbon and the order's share of all the other operating costs of the business are taken into account the net profit on this order will be about £2 at best.

Steve walks into shop B and is met by a smiling Pippa. Like Dave he knows next to nothing about flowers and is also nervous about displaying his ignorance. He met Jane two months ago and is madly in love with her. He wants to impress her and convince her about just how deeply he feels for her.

'How much is a bouquet?' Steve asks nervously.

Pippa smiles. 'Well it depends on the occasion really and how much you'd like to spend. Bouquets range in price from £20 for the most basic through to £150 for the most luxurious.'

'Wow, £150 is out of my league, but I do want to make an impression and I definitely don't want something that looks bargain basement' Steve replies.

'Can I ask what the occasion is?' smiles Pippa.

Steve decides Pippa looks friendly and understanding and he tells her about Jane. Pippa suggests that a nice hand-tied bouquet might be more appropriate and shows him one she has just made. Steve is suitably impressed and asks how much it is.

Pippa tells him that it is £50 and also shows him a £20 gift wrap so he can see the difference. Steve immediately opts for the hand-tied and tells her that really, he isn't all that bothered by the cost if he can just make the desired impression on the lovely Jane.

Pippa laughs and says she loves it when her boyfriend really wants to impress her.

'So, what would really impress you' asks Steve, confident that he now has a little bit of rapport with this nice friendly lady.

'Well, what would really, really impress me would be a bouquet like this and a bottle of bubbly and, if he wanted to really push the boat out, some chocolates would be lovely.'

'Do you sell those too?' asks Steve.

Five minutes later Steve leaves the shop having spent £87.99 and he has a big smile on his face. He is convinced that Jane will be super impressed and he has Pippa's business card in his wallet. He knows who to talk to when it is Jane's birthday in three months time and also when it comes to Valentines Day.

Because of the different metrics of this order the net profit for the shop when all the sums are done is over £15.

I have so often been in a florist shop when a customer has asked the 'how much is a bouquet' question and I fervently believe that the response tells you so much about that shop. The 'Marjorie' shops display a lack of drive and weak management and training – typically they make little money. The 'Pippa' shops show what is possible with some dynamism and inter-personal skills and are usually way more profitable.

I believe this is the easiest way to improve the profitability of any floristry business. It is easy to increase the average sale and it is one of the rare occasions when you can actually make the customer feel better after having spent more than they initially intended.

If the customer doesn't want anything more than a basic gift-wrap this is fine – BUT always tell the customer what the options are. Some florists seem to think it is being pushy to suggest extras but I don't agree. Whenever I buy anything I want to know how my purchase might be improved.

If I book a hotel room on the coast and there is an option to pay an extra £10 to get a sea-view room, then I want to know about this. I would be annoyed to arrive and get a room overlooking the back yard and then have the receptionist tell me that I could have had a sea-view but unfortunately all of those rooms are now reserved.

A well designed and constructed website also gives the same opportunity as it can show the full range of options and suggest what is appropriate for different occasions. Amazon's 'customers who bought x also bought y' is an excellent example of just how effective this approach is. Their sales are massively increased by customers taking note of this and ordering extra items.

Another big benefit of selling via the Internet is that on your website your business can be open 24 hours a day, 365 days a year. It's lovely gathering new orders while you are asleep!

I know that I keep promoting the Internet but I make no apologies for this. Like it or loathe it, it is not just the future, it is today! If you think you can avoid it you will have to be a miracle worker to prosper without it.

Another important message about selling is to treat everyone the same. Don't assume that some customers are wealthy and some are poor. I have seen some very scruffy customers turn out to be really big spenders! As an example, I have seen a florist take a phone call from someone enquiring about a funeral tribute and they are only told about the cost of a basic small spray. When I asked why the florist replied 'oh, she was probably a little old lady and has to live on her pension.'

When a smart middle-aged lady pulls up in front of the shop in a new Mercedes to collect her little spray you realise that you should never make assumptions like that. Tell people the options and they can choose whether to spend £20 or £200.

Advertising

Soon after acquiring our first shop we spent a weekend in Birmingham attending the Spring Florist Event for the first time. We were both very inexperienced and were keen not just to visit all the stands but to talk to lots of people whom we felt we could learn from. Associated workshops were run, focussing on different aspects of the floristry trade. While Liz attended all the design demonstrations I attended the more general business sessions.

One of these sessions addressed sales and marketing and included an open forum. As someone who was at that time entrenched in the I.T. industry, and completely new to the floristry world, I was very keen to know how best we should spend our little marketing budget. Finding myself in a room full of experienced shop owners I asked them all what they felt was the most effective form of marketing.

The response I received was absolutely unanimous in that everyone felt that print advertising was a waste of money. The Internet was relatively new in those days but already people were starting to invest in that sector. People who had for many years spent money on adverts in Yellow Pages or Thomsons were switching that money to Internet advertising.

We then pretty much followed this advice to the letter. We did occasionally try a little advertising in the local press but it was indeed a waste of money.

I had some flyers and discount cards printed at very low cost by a friend who owned a printing business. We hand delivered 5,000 of these through local letterboxes. These cards gave the holder a 10 per cent discount and they were quite effective, with some customers continuing to use them for several years. However, if we had had to pay the true cost of printing, this exercise would not have been cost effective.

In the early days we did try cold calling prospects by phone and quite frankly we found this to be a depressing and largely fruitless exercise. I know this must work for some industries or else the double-glazing trade wouldn't invest so much money in it, but I don't believe it works for florists. I know I just hate to be cold called at home so I didn't blame anyone who hung up on me!

Telesales

For most florists telesales means receiving inbound calls from customers. This is very different from outbound calls, where you are hoping there is a slight chance that the person you are calling may be interested in what you have to offer.

Inbound calls typically come from people who have already decided to buy and are calling to place their order. We found that 90 per cent of inbound calls resulted in an order. Those who did not order were often people who thought they could have a bouquet delivered for £15 or less and couldn't imagine spending more than that on flowers.

The impact you make when receiving an inbound call depends on just how you handle it. As mentioned earlier one florist may take a £20 order whilst another florist taking the exact same call might have trebled or quadrupled the order value. This really is of enormous importance and is the key to improving the performance of a business.

I found Interflora very helpful in providing their preferred sales script to all their member shops and our telephone sales technique was often tested by them. They would phone us pretending to be a customer and record the call. We would then receive a copy of the recording together with an assessment report.

I believe that the ideal script is slightly different from the Interflora recommendation. I learned from professional telesales trainers that the sequence and structure of taking a call is crucially important.

An example of my favoured script is as follows:

'Good morning, Biggs Florist, how can I help you?'

Do not say the business name first as many callers do not take in the first one or two words of your response.

'Can I take a contact telephone number for you please, Mr. Smith?'

Customers are more inclined to proceed with an order if they know you have a means of contacting them. As a form of address you should usually use whatever means of address the customer themselves used. If the customer identifies himself as John Smith then call him John, but if he says Mr. Smith then call him Mr. Smith. This can vary with some customers, however, and you have to use your discretion. You can probably tell from Mary Smith's tone of voice whether or not she is likely to prefer to be called Mrs. Smith.

'When would you like this delivered?'

Check both the day and the date.

'Can I please take the name and address of the recipient, Mr. Smith?'

Again, taking address details at an early stage increases the likelihood that the caller will proceed with an order.

'What would you like to order?'

'Bouquets range in price from £20 for the smallest to £150 for the largest and most luxurious. May I ask what the occasion is?'

'For a silver wedding anniversary people typically spend at least £60 on the bouquet to get something really special.'

'We do also sell very nice helium balloons with a 'Congratulations on your Silver Wedding' message. This could be attached to the bouquet and would cost an extra £5.'

'We also sell other extras like champagne and chocolates for very special occasions.'

'What message would you like to go on a card to be attached to the flowers?'

'So that will be a total of £99.95 to cover the bouquet, a balloon, chocolates and delivery.'

Do not mention the delivery charge until you reach this stage and state it in a matter of fact way, as it is a standard part of the order. Never say it in an apologetic way or suggest that it might be open to negotiation.

'How would you like to pay? We accept all major credit and debit cards.'

Take the card type, number, expiry date and the last three digits of the number on the signature strip on the back of the card.

'May I please take the address that your card statements are sent to?'

'Thank you for your order Mr. Smith. The amount of £99.95 will be debited from your account. I will ensure that we deliver your order on Wednesday, 15th. March.'

When we first became Interflora members I remember attending their new members course. One session on telesales was given by a director who had built up a large and very successful florist telesales business. He stated that the least successful telesales operators he had ever employed were florists as they were so inept at selling upwards. Please ensure you don't fall in to the trap of taking the easy way out and always assuming the

85

customer wants the most basic option. Think about the massive improvement increased order values make to your profits.

We introduced an incentive scheme for our staff that related to the average value of all the orders we took. Before long people who had previously been selling lots of £20 gift-wrapped bouquets were boasting about the size of their order each time they put the phone down.

There was much good-natured banter as the details of big sales were broadcast around the workroom and there was much mickey-taking each time someone took a small order with no add-ons.

It is of course vitally important to be just as courteous when the customer only wants to spend the minimum amount. It is possible to leave the customer feeling good about the way you handled their order, no matter how much they spent. The key thing is to let them know the options and let the customer make up their own mind. Somebody who places a small order today may place bigger orders in the future.

Distance & online selling regulations

Any business that gives customers the opportunity to buy via a distance or online transaction must adhere to the appropriate government regulations.

Distance selling is the sale of goods or services through digital TV, mail order, phone or text. If you don't follow the rules the penalties can be severe, including the payment of compensation, an unlimited fine or prison!

The regulations specify the details you must provide to the customer before an order is placed, the customers right to cancel and what you must do after the order is placed. At the time of writing these regulations apply to every transaction to the value of more than £42. All the current regulations can be found at https://www.gov.uk/online-and-distance-selling-forbusinesses/online-selling

In addition to the rules for distance selling there are extra rules for selling online. The government website also specifies the rules relating to VAT, data protection and sales to other EU countries.

Sales within a shop

When the customer is actually present in a shop the sales approach should be similar to the telesales example we covered. However, shop sales can be personalised much more. There is the opportunity to really build a rapport by learning and using the names of regular customers, chatting about the occasion, favourite colours, allergies to certain flowers and known preferences.

In our shop when customers needed to wait for something to be made, they could sit on a sofa and we would offer them tea or coffee while they read a newspaper or a magazine.

It is so important to greet any customer entering the shop. Even if the only member of staff present is halfway through making a hand-tied bouquet they can still say 'Hello' and smile welcomingly. The customer will almost invariably be understanding. In fact we often found the customer was interested in watching the make-up work while they waited and would sometimes request something similar to be made for them.

Even if someone entering the shop is only seeking directions it pays to be pleasant and helpful. If you go out of your way to help they will remember this and may become a customer in the future.

Once a lady was taken ill outside our shop. We helped her inside, sat her down and made her a cup of tea while we phoned her husband. We only did what most people would have done but they became good customers from that day on.

One very useful thing we did was to file all the old orders so we could easily refer back to them if need be. A customer might call to say he wanted an anniversary bouquet for his wife. He wanted an exact repeat of what we had delivered the year before but could not describe what it was. We would find the order from the previous year and be able to find out just what we had put in to it.

Many businesses now maintain a customer database that includes details of birthdays and anniversaries. The computer might notify you that Mr. Smith's wedding anniversary is coming up next week. If he hasn't ordered anything yet a friendly reminder by phone call or email can win an order.

If he says he is taking Mrs. Smith away somewhere and will not need flowers this year then no problem. You can say you just wanted to check he hadn't forgotten and you didn't want him to get into trouble. You could take the opportunity to offer to arrange for flowers to be placed in their hotel room. Many people love this sort of special service and are happy to pay for it. It makes them feel that you are acknowledging them as a good customer, deserving of special treatment.

We have already mentioned that men are often embarrassed when walking in to a florist shop and not really knowing what to buy. It is best for the salesperson to lead the conversation and make appropriate suggestions. In fact this type of sale is an excellent opportunity for a high value order based on what stock is currently available.

Different people have different tastes. If a customer insisted on a strange mix of flowers wrapped in what our girls referred to as 'prostitute pink' cellophane, then that is what they got, even if the florists had a quiet laugh while making it up.

We had one customer who wanted one dead flower delivered to his girl-friend at her office at 10am. This was to be followed by ten dozen red roses to be delivered at 11am. We made sure that when we did the first delivery there was nothing with the shop name on it!

When the customer is actually present in the shop the easiest way is often to show them examples of high value orders that have just been made up. Frequently the customer will say 'That looks great, I'll have one of those please'. Then the opportunity exists to show them add-ons which can further enhance the order.

All staff should be smart and consistent in their appearance. A uniform appearance can be maintained by giving each member of staff a clean tabard, with the shop's name on and also perhaps the name of the relay service the shop belongs to.

Make the most of the added opportunities to sell cards, vases, glassware and assorted giftware. Often customers will wander around your shop while they wait for their order to be made up and it is a great opportunity for impulse sales.

We had links with some local artists and would display their work around the shop, using a 100 per cent mark-up on their work. This resulted in only occasional sales but it enhanced the overall appearance of the shop too.

Flower subscriptions

One relatively new trend is for customers to sign up to a regular delivery of flowers. This could be weekly, fortnightly or monthly.

Pioneered by companies such as Bloom & Wild – the focus was on flowers delivered by post but now the likes of FLOWERBX also offer a similar service delivered directly to customers in London.

It isn't something that only a specialist subscription service can offer though. Just about any floristry business can offer subscriptions to their customer base. You could try offering this service on your website and within your shop. A home florist can offer this to their local customer base.

This is a good example of why you should keep tabs on what everyone else is doing. You may come across some new niche in the market and realise you couldn't possible do that but often there is absolutely no reason why you can't. Don't just assume that a slick new operator has appeared on the scene and they will already have cornered the market with their idea. Anything like this takes a long time to get established and to develop into a viable business so why not try offering it and see what response you get.

Keeping tabs on competitors

No matter how well your business is performing you can never ignore what your competitors are doing. Learn what you can from your visiting wholesalers but take what they say with a pinch of salt. Some florists will only tell their wholesalers things which they actually want to get passed on. Wholesalers often form their own view of how a particular business is doing by what they buy and how busy they appear to be.

We always found that most wholesalers loved a good gossip. If you were friendly towards them and made them a cup of tea it was possible to learn all sorts of interesting things.

If your competitors are doing some sort of special promotion or changing their method of advertising then you need to know. If they need more or fewer staff it is an indicator of how well they are doing.

Often wholesalers will moan about how long it was taking them to get paid by a particular business. Sometimes they would tell stories about a business that might have owed them thousands of pounds for over six months. All of this information helps you to assess the competition and ensure that you are poised to take advantage of any opportunities that may arise if a nearby business suddenly closes down.

I found two situations like this in Cambridge and agreed a deal with the failing businesses, whereby we would take over all their customer base, including all their contract customers. The key thing in this situation is to get in first!

If a competitor changes their delivery charges, or offers a later cut-off time for same day orders, you want to know before a customer tells you. If a competitor starts to promote free delivery you will want to counter this. You might explain that 'free delivery' often means fewer flowers going in to each order to cover the cost of delivery.

It is also good to keep an objective eye on the quality levels of other shops. When delivering to a funeral director I would always have a good look at the items that had been delivered by other florists. I found there was a general correlation between the quality of each business's products and the general perception of that business. Shops that had a reputation for being cheap and cheerful did indeed deliver products that reflected this. Shops with a quality image and a good reputation consistently delivered good work and good quality flowers.

Business hours

Opening hours will depend on many different factors. To some extent you need to fit in with other shops in the immediate vicinity If your shop is in a town centre or in a parade then customers will expect all the shops to keep similar hours.

On weekdays we officially opened from 8.30am to 5pm but in practice we were almost always open from 8am because this is when we usually arrived. There always seemed to be early deliveries to make and we were keen to get ready for the day ahead. We usually closed late, either because we had late customers or we were still tidying up at the end of the day. We took the view that if we were there we might as well be open!

On Mondays and Saturdays our Dutch wholesaler delivered at 6am so we opened really early. Ideally we should have stayed open until 6pm to catch all the end of day opportunities, as working customers were on their way home, but we felt our day was long enough as it was. Had we ever fallen on hard times we knew that staying open an extra hour would boost sales. On a Saturday we closed at 4.30pm. Although we didn't get many walk-in customers on a Saturday afternoon we usually had appointments booked for wedding consultations. Also we started make-up work on a Saturday afternoon for the weekly office deliveries that had to be made early on Monday morning.

Florists are usually open for business every day of the year except for Sundays and public holidays. The main exceptions are of course Mother's Day and Valentine's Day.

At Easter we found that if we opened on Good Friday sales were typically about half of a normal days's trading. Opening on either Easter Sunday or Monday was a complete waste of time and after trying this once or twice we gave up. Sales on the Saturday of Easter weekend were usually slightly better than a normal Saturday.

Many florists will close for the whole of the period between Christmas Day through to New Year's Day but we never did. We actually found that sales were very good in that week as we were just about the only florist open in the area. We would take a number of funeral orders for the backlog of funerals which always builds up over the Christmas period. Also there were so many people on holiday who were tired of eating, drinking and watching TV and just wanted to get out and do some shopping. The biggest problem was finding a wholesaler who could deliver in that week but we always managed to find fresh stock from somewhere.

Customer confidentiality

Discretion is obviously vitally important because of the very personal nature of many orders and their accompanying messages. A florist is frequently asked to promise the customer that they will not divulge the sender's name, or any other details, to the recipient.

At Valentine's Day we always received a number of calls from people pleading with us to divulge the sender's details but unless we could get the sender's permission we would not do so. Often when calling the customer in this type of situation we would find they had given us a false name or telephone number anyway. The only exception we ever made was to provide details to the police if they requested them, and even then, we needed to be satisfied about what they would do with this information.

Some recipients will ask you to tell them where the order came from. If it is a relay order they want to know which town it was sent from. You should never divulge even this much information as often this is sufficient for them to work out who their flowers were from.

We once received a very hostile call from a school headmistress demanding to know why we had delivered red roses to a fourteen year old pupil. It turned out that they were from a forty year old man who had been stalking the girl. We explained that we had no way of knowing this: she could have been a teacher or anyone working at the school.

At the end of one Valentine Day, after we had finally locked the doors, a lady repeatedly knocked . She demanded to know who her flowers were from and said she would not leave until we told her. After we politely refused she produced her warrant card – she was an off-duty policewoman. We still didn't tell her because the sender had been adamant about his anonymity.

It was not uncommon for ladies to tell us they must find out whether their flowers were from their husband or their boyfriend. They needed to know what to say, or not say, when they got home.

It can be quite amusing when people place multiple orders for flowers to go to different people on Valentine's Day. I remember once taking an order from a small bespectacled man in a three-piece suit. He sent six bouquets to six different ladies, all with quite racy messages!

You should never knowingly allow a customer to send a message containing obscene words and I have known people who wanted to. It is a matter of discretion that sometimes you need to suggest some more appropriate wording.

Networking

Networking is something that every florist will do every day by simply talking to people. However, it can pay to join a more formal networking group to promote your business.

I belonged to the Cambridge branch of BNI (Business Network International), which I found to be very effective. A group of some forty people representing all sorts of businesses would meet at the ungodly hour of 6.30am every Tuesday. After a working breakfast, we then had a strictly timetabled meeting that lasted from 7am to 8.30am.

Each member had a 60 second slot in which to promote their business and make it as interesting as possible. This meant new ideas, funny stories, songs, poems or anything that grabbed peoples attention and made them aware of your business.

The idea was that all the members of the group would positively promote all the other members' products and services. Only one member of each profession was involved in a single chapter of the organisation. As the only 'florist' I worked together with a printer, insurance broker, cake maker, carpet cleaner, website designer, leaflet distributor, courier service, driving instructor, solicitor, estate agent, accountant, sign-writer and many others, to learn about what they offered.

The most important part of the meeting was the referrals section. In the previous week every member was expected to find at least one business opportunity for one of the other members of the group. One week I might pass on the details of someone I knew who wanted their carpets cleaning and the next it would be the details of somebody whose car insurance was coming up for renewal.

Continually finding these referrals was hard work but it was what made the whole venture function. Every week I left the meeting with at least one order for flowers and at peak periods I always left with several.

Like so many things in life, what you get out of these networking groups depends on what you put into it. Some people found it incredibly difficult to drag themselves out of bed for a 6.30am meeting. As a morning person, who always liked to get to the shop early, this was never a problem for me.

Each week one member had a ten-minute slot in which to promote their business in a little more detail. Fortunately my turn came the week before Valentine's Day. After explaining all the 'specials' we were promoting, I gave each member a red rose. I also gave the winner of the weekly raffle an impressive hand-tied bouquet. I left that meeting with lots of orders.

There are various similar networking organisations, including the Chamber of Commerce, and I would recommend you to check on what exists in your local area.

Apart from the many orders we received through BNI we also got lots of good PR. I loved all the occasions when another member would stand up and tell the whole meeting that our shop had provided flowers for their wife/mother/whoever and that they were fantastic.

The annual membership fee for a networking group is typically about four hundred pounds but I found it was hard to get better value than this from my marketing budget.

Weddings

Any floristry business is likely to be targeted by anyone putting on a wedding fair. These events are usually held in a local hotel where the suppliers of wedding services can promote their services to couples planning their big day.

Wedding fairs can be quite expensive because, in addition to the fee charged by the organisers, you will incur a variety of further costs. You have to provide the flowers, accessories and labour used to make up whatever you choose to put on show. Then you have to provide labour to man the stand on the day.

You will need to win bookings for several weddings to cover the costs of the event and enable you to make a reasonable profit. Of course, once in a while you might get lucky and land one or two really big multi-thousand pound weddings which make it all well worthwhile.

The majority of florists consider these fairs to be a waste of time and money. We considered that we won enough wedding orders through our other marketing efforts and, very importantly, by word of mouth recommendations and so we felt we didn't need to attend wedding fairs. The average return on the investment required is usually very small and often they result in a financial loss.

What we did find very useful was a link with the Cambridge branch of Debenhams, who did attend many of the local wedding fairs. In return for us supplying sample wedding arrangements for them to display within the store and at fairs, they promoted our services. They also supplied us with mannequins and wedding dresses that we used in our window displays. This was a good arrangement with both parties benefitting from each other.

As with funeral arrangements, we designated one area of the shop for customers to sit down with a florist, and look at our albums of work that we had done in the past. There was also one album containing the many thank-you letters we had received from brides, grooms and parents. This area also had examples of bride's bouquets etc. made from artificial flowers and there were many wedding books and magazines for stimulating ideas.

Following the wedding consultation, we would provide a detailed price quotation. If the customer wanted to make a firm booking we requested a £50 non-refundable deposit and the balance for the full amount was due two weeks prior to the date of the wedding.

We had one very strange wedding order that worried and completely baffled us. The bride-to-be made several visits to the shop to discuss her wedding plans and to check every last detail. She paid the full price, in advance, in cash, and we duly ordered the flowers and made everything she had requested. Then we attempted to deliver everything on the big day.

When we called at the address she had given us, the occupants of the house declared that they didn't know anyone by that name and they didn't know of anyone getting married that day. We rang the phone number she had given us but only got the 'number unobtainable' tone. She had also given us an address for the groom and wanted corsages etc. delivered there, but we found the house number simply didn't exist.

By now we were really panicking as we assumed we had made a number of terrible mistakes when taking down all the details. We told ourselves that surely she would phone any minute demanding to know where her flowers were.

We didn't get any phone call and we never saw her or heard from her ever again. The flowers sat in the cold room for a couple of weeks until eventually we threw them out. It was a mystery which we never got to the bottom of. Whether her whole wedding plan was some strange fantasy we never knew but it certainly distressed us at the time.

One last word on weddings is to beware of the bride's mother! During the wedding consultations we often found the bride's mother to be much more difficult to deal with than the bride and groom. On one occasion the mother didn't let the bride get a word in edgeways and told her daughter what she should have. The bride then returned to the shop later, on her own, saying that she would like to start again and tell us what she wanted!

Funerals

Sympathy work will always be a significant part of the day-to-day sales for any florist. It is tempting to seek a deal with local funeral directors and there is no doubt many of them will actively pursue floristry opportunities in return for a cut of the proceeds.

Quite what percentage a funeral director will seek varies enormously and I know of florists who have agreed to anything between 10 and 25 per cent. Some will pursue this business very proactively – with professionally produced guides featuring excellent photographs of all their different offerings. They may also provide sympathy card stands and examples of their work made up in silk.

I think a commission arrangement of up to 15 percent can make this a good deal but any more than that and it is seriously eating into the profit margin.

We always found that we received a healthy level of funeral work anyway and consequently I didn't go looking for deals with a funeral director.

One of the attractions is of course that you can use older stock for much of your sympathy work while still providing an attractive product that is fresh enough to please the customer.

Signage

When we took over both of our shops they had very poor, old-fashioned signage on both the shop itself and on the delivery vans. One of our first tasks was to replace these as quickly as possible. Bold, fresh signage over the shop is absolutely essential. Once you have that in place you must make the effort to keep it clean at all times. As the old saying goes, you never get a second chance to make a first impression.

The single best marketing investment we ever made was to spend £570 on each of the two vans at the Cambridge shop. For this, we had on each side of the vans a very striking photograph of a hand-tied bouquet and the shop name, address, phone number, website address and Interflora logo. Most of the population of Cambridge seemed to know about us as the vans made such an impression around the city.

Away from the shop, whenever anyone asked us what we did and we told them we owned Biggs Florist, they would tell us they had seen our vans. Even the Yellow Pages rep told us he thought the vans were probably ten times more effective than anything else we were spending our marketing money on.

Before many people enter a shop, they will look at the windows or the shop door, to see which credit/debit cards are accepted and so it is important to use the stickers provided by the card companies.

Customers also expect you to display the shop opening hours and to be open when you say you are going to be. You will lose some customers for ever if it isn't, even if you display a sign saying 'Back in ten minutes'. You might get away with this in a remote location where you are the only florist but it is the kiss of death in a busy town centre.

Shop layout

Layout will largely depend on the space you have but it is a good idea to decide on the sort of image you want to project. If you display absolutely everything and leave little space for customers to walk around this can project an uninviting, cluttered image. It doesn't encourage customers to spend much time browsing.

I am always amazed when shopkeepers, with limited available space, display lots of identical items. It is far better to display just one or two examples of each item. Advertisers always talk about the effective use of white space in an advert and I think the same principle applies in a shop.

Minimalism can be taken too far, of course, as you don't want customers to gain the impression that you only have a very limited range. If you are not displaying many fresh flowers because the weather is hot, and most stock is in the cold room, then let your customers know this. This is an opportunity to impress and inform your customers, who then know you have the facilities to prolong the life of whatever they are buying.

Chilled display cabinets in the shop can provide the best of both worlds but they are very expensive and have limited space. If your walk-in trade is big enough then you may be able to cost-justify this.

As supermarkets demonstrate, the choice of what to display near the point of sale is very important. It makes sense to use this area to display add-ons such as chocolates, teddies, a balloon stand, a greeting card stand and even champagne if you have a licence.

You must have a licence to sell wine and champagne – this involves a small fee, some form filling, a one-day training course and a court appearance.

Changing the window display regularly can be a chore but we always tried to change ours completely every two weeks. I was surprised at how many people took the time to take a good look at the windows, even when the shop was closed. If you fail to do something special for each of the peak periods then people think that you are not making enough of an effort.

Having fresh flowers in the window is crucial, even though you have to bear the cost of wastage and you will want to keep them out of direct sunlight. Having only artificial flowers on display may save money but does not project the best image. It is worth accepting some wastage to tempt in the majority of people who like to see high quality fresh flowers.

Some florists like to display lots of fresh flowers outside the shop. This can look very attractive and is likely to entice more passing trade but unfortunately this can significantly shorten product life. Flowers do not like traffic fumes and extreme temperatures.

Keeping stock inside the shop, or better still in a cold room, will greatly reduce wastage and the ideal situation is probably a compromise. Only put out the stock you are confident will sell that day. If the passing trade isn't buying it quickly enough then give it to the florists for current make-up work.

Dealing with your competitors

We mentioned before the importance of keeping tabs on your competitors and taking advantage if one of them should close. As well as doing a deal with a failing business to acquire their customer base you can also arrange to have their inbound phone calls diverted to your business.

Most florists are on good terms with their local competitors as there are many occasions where they can help each other out. We frequently contacted other florists if we were in urgent need of something and they did the same when they had a problem. We might have suddenly needed open lilies for a funeral order, or perhaps a particular oasis frame. We were always happy to help other florists and we regularly begged and borrowed from each other. If you decide all your competitors are enemies, as some florists do, it is unlikely to be in your best interests.

When one of our competitors closed I have explained that I moved very quickly to do a deal with them and would make sure I was present when they closed their doors for the last time. The proprietor called the phone company to terminate their lines and then handed the phone to me so I could arrange to have all their calls diverted to us. It is so important to do this quickly as there are telesales businesses all around the country that seek opportunities like this.

I then contacted all their contract customers to let them know the business had closed but that we had reached an agreement with the owner to take over their account. We would promise to provide them with the same service at the same price. This may seem mercenary but if the owner has already decided to shut up shop they will welcome the opportunity to at least make a little money by selling their customer base as they close their doors for the final time.

There can, however, be problems related to the type of service that has previously been provided by a business that has closed. One small shop that had been our nearest competitor failed largely because they provided flowers at incredibly low prices. Also they often included free delivery and could not possibly run at a profit.

When their calls were diverted to us we were often asked to deliver the impossible. People would ask for a large bouquet for a total of £15, including free delivery. We then had to explain that we were very sorry but we were unable to do this. Most customers would listen to the reasons, accept them and go ahead with an order anyway. A small minority would not listen and accused us of charging extortionate prices. Those were the customers we decided we couldn't afford to placate.

Conversely another shop that closed was located in a very affluent part of Cambridge. We found that most of their customers were used to spending considerably more than the average. The order volumes were not huge but the order values were excellent.

Sales and marketing – checklist

- Focus on maximising every sale
- Always explain the options
- Never assume the customer is poor!
- Focus your advertising on the Internet
- Develop a telesales script
- Comply with online selling regulations
- Consider new ideas like subscriptions
- Develop a customer database
- Pamper your best customers
- Learn from your wholesalers
- Optimise your opening hours
- Maintain customer confidentiality
- Join a networking group
- Invest in impressive signage
- Streamline your shop layout
- Develop a rapport with your competitors

6 Buying stock

This chapter addresses:

- Where to buy
- Cooperative ventures
- Conditioning the stock
- Wastage
- Mark-ups and pricing
- Marking up on non-floral products
- Peak periods
- Giving products away

The buying of stock is one of the most crucial aspects of any type of floristry business and it is one over which an owner should have a great deal of influence. You may feel that you have little flexibility for cutting the costs of many of the general operating expenses such as rent, business rates and utilities. However you can have an enormous impact on what you spend on stock, how you care for that stock and what price you sell it for.

Liz did most of the buying for our shops and when she became ill Jo, the shop manager, took on that role. They focussed on ensuring we bought whatever we needed, from the best suppliers we could find, to fulfil all the orders. While they checked all the stock for quality and anticipated vase life, I spent a lot of time on the financial aspects of stock purchasing.

I found from experience that it was naïve to simply assume that all of the listed wholesale prices were set in stone. Two different florists can pay quite different sums for their stock and the impact on your profit can vary considerably.

Where to buy

Most florists will rely largely on the different wholesale suppliers who visit their area. Depending on the location, most retailers will have a range of primarily Dutch suppliers visiting them on a regular basis. There may be a few local wholesalers who also visit and most of these will typically specialise in plants and sundries.

The Dutch suppliers normally use a large refrigerated lorry that they fill with fresh flowers, foliage and plants. We used suppliers who bought and loaded at the Dutch auctions. They would cross the channel overnight and call on us and other Cambridge florists early the following morning.

Once the different shops in Cambridge had all been visited the wholesaler would venture further afield, spending several days visiting lots of florists across East Anglia and the south east before heading back to Holland. They would often have an arrangement whereby they offloaded all their remaining stock to someone at a very low price before leaving the country.

Often these job lots of stock end up being sold from a van at the side of the road or on a market stall. It can be very frustrating for a florist to be challenged by a customer over why their prices are far higher than those on a market stall. We used to take the time to explain that the flowers bought cheaply in the market had often been on a lorry for several days and had been rejected by the many florists the wholesaler had visited. The wholesaler could either throw them away or get whatever price they could for them. There are always people prepared to take someones old stock if they think they can make an easy profit. But the rule is inescapable: by and large you get what you pay for.

Many of our customers were very interested to hear this sort of thing. It reinforced their decision to buy their flowers from a proper florist. It made them more likely to feel that they were buying wisely.

We always found that the local wholesalers provided a good, reliable service but they had great difficulty competing with the prices that the Dutchmen could offer. Most of the local wholesalers that we used regularly were specialists in one particular sector, some in plants, some in accessories and sundries, and some in giftware such as pots and vases.

A constant problem is the way the Dutch price their stock. We found that different shops were charged very different prices. Occasionally we would phone some of our local competitors and swap information about what each of us had been charged that day by a particular supplier.

Some differential pricing can be justified because a large shop, consistently buying large volumes, can expect to receive some sort of volume discount. However, some pricing can be purely opportunistic. Hard-nosed hagglers can pay significantly less than pleasant, friendly florists who simply accept whatever prices they are charged. If you hate to haggle you can always smile and say to a wholesaler 'of course, I always compare notes with the other florists you go to'.

One of the Dutch wholesalers we used gave us intimate access to the internal part of their website. We could not only check on their pricing but also find out what they had paid for the stock at the Aalsmeer auction. This supplier also listed the prices by stem on the shelves in the lorry. This made it easy for florists to know what the current prices were and then decide whether or not to buy.

Other suppliers would fax us their current price list the day before calling on us so we could plan our purchasing ahead. This was a great help and solved the problem of what to do when a wholesaler called and you felt some of the prices were too high. If no other supplier is calling that day you might have to buy anyway to fulfil your orders and to comply with the range of stock your relay service provider requires you to have.

The buying process is usually a difficult balance of gauging prices against quality levels. We found that often a new wholesaler would visit us offering very impressive prices and excellent quality but that unfortunately they could not maintain this over a period of time. Either prices would creep up and/or quality levels would dip and you began to suspect they were selling some old stock.

With some suppliers, we found that entering into any sort of volume purchasing agreement was actually a bad idea. Although the prices dropped, they began to rely on us buying in large volume and the quality levels would drop.

Some florists are prepared to get out of bed in the middle of the night and drive to market to buy their stock. If you are experienced enough to know that you are buying the best quality at the best prices this can result in huge savings. However, if you are not so experienced it is easy to pay over the odds and lose a lot of sleep for very little return.

I have always been very impressed by some experienced florists who get up at 3am, drive to New Covent Garden, do all their buying and then unload the flowers at their shop before working a full day. I have to say that we never had that much energy. We were quite happy to have wholesalers delivering just about everything we needed, even if it meant accepting a lower level of profit.

Had Liz and I entered the floristry trade when we were in our twenties or thirties things might have been different. We would have had the drive and the energy to buy regularly at market because we would have been hungry for the extra profit.

Another method of buying is to do it all over the internet and have stock delivered directly. It might come direct from the markets or even directly from growers. This is buying stock in much the same way as many people purchase their groceries these days.

When we tried to do this we met with a number of problems, usually related to the method of delivery. Delivery is usually made by some sort of generalised delivery service, rather than by anyone with a specialised knowledge of flowers and their care. Consequently we had problems with deliveries arriving out of shop hours. Some of the stock was delivered in a nonrefrigerated lorry and we had difficulties with returning trolleys and containers to suppliers. One supplier charged us a deposit for the trolleys and for each of the buckets delivered to us. We then experienced all sorts of problems with getting these deposits correctly credited back to us when we returned them.

Levels of service for this sort of on-line buying are however improving significantly now through businesses like Floribest and floradirect. They have learnt from experience how to organise the logistics of buying and transporting flowers in a way that causes florists the least amount of hassle. They enable you to enter your requirements online and they then compare the stock and prices of all the exporters on their system. You can choose the variety, stem length, price, quality, exporter and even grower.

This method enables you to get low prices and if you order before 2pm you can get next-day doorstep delivery by 10am. floradirect have a team of people in Holland at the point where the flowers are bought and despatched. They utilise a freight and transportation operation which is experienced in delivering flowers in excellent condition.

In a nutshell, we found through experience that the best method was to use a combination of online buying and also a small group of visiting wholesalers. These were people who were tried and tested and who we had come to trust over a period of time. Good communication is essential so that when you have a genuine gripe there is no need to bang the table to get a fair resolution. Of course, it has to be a two-way relationship and if you are a reliable and prompt payer then you should find your wholesalers will respect you and want to work with you through the good times and the bad.

109

Cooperative ventures

Another means of buying stock is to enter into some form of cooperative venture with other florists. We did try this but I have to admit it was not a success. I will describe how this works only to provide a warning to anyone considering this type of venture.

We joined a cooperative of independent florists to set up a business that would enable us to buy flowers directly from the Dutch auctions. They would be delivered directly to each member shop in our own refrigerated lorry. The business hired a buyer-driver and leased a suitably sized lorry. We all entered into it with high hopes of greatly reduced prices and better quality flowers. To make this cooperative work it needed a core of some 25 members. This would enable us all to make significant savings if the concept proved workable. We were sceptical from the outset but the potential savings looked so attractive that we decided to give it a try.

The first deliveries were fraught with problems, mainly due to logistics, as we all had to work to such tight deadlines. The driver needed to fit in the buying, loading, ferry journeys and delivering across an area covering London to Yorkshire. After the first month things improved a little but there were still many problems. It seemed that we had not been told the whole truth about exactly how many members had committed to the scheme and paid their share of the start-up costs.

It soon became obvious that there were fewer than the 25 members required in the business plan. This meant members were being asked to pay slightly more per stem to make up the shortfall. Some members decided at an early stage that the concept would never work and pulled out. Before long there were more shops pulling out than there were new members joining and the whole venture collapsed.

It was a shame this scheme didn't work because for a short spell, after the initial teething problems, it looked as though it might. We were receiving deliveries of excellent quality flowers at the lowest prices we had ever achieved. The whole venture lasted only a few months.

When I came to do all the sums after we had pulled out I found that we had still made a small saving when everything was taken into account. However, these figures didn't take into account the many meetings we attended and the time taken trying to manage the problems we experienced. So we took the view that although it had been an interesting exercise, which had not actually lost us any money, we would never venture into such a scheme ever again.

I am told by some wholesalers and shop owners that other similar schemes have been tried before but that all of them have failed, usually because of the problems involved in getting enough businesses signed up and sufficiently committed to making it work.

Conditioning the stock

Probably the least popular job in floristry is conditioning the stock once it arrives. This involves stripping off the leaves and thorns, cutting the stems and getting the flowers into water. Although this is a very important task it is usually considered to be very boring work and it can be extremely tiring.

Oasis claim to have significantly reduced the drudgery of conditioning work with their Flora Express no-cut product. I am told that this really does work and has been thoroughly tested. The idea of not having to cut all those thousands of stems seems like a florist's dream.

It is also very important to regularly clean all the buckets and vases with bleach and water. Then they should be thoroughly rinsed out with fresh water. If this is not done, bacteria can rapidly kill off your stock.

I know of one shop where the new owner asked his florists what he could do to help out. They replied that bleaching the vases was always a great help to them. At the end of the day, when all the staff had gone home, he went around the shop pouring neat bleach into each and every vase. When the florists arrived the following morning they found that all the stock had died overnight!

As part of the conditioning work we would randomly check the number of stems in each wrap or bunch of flowers. Often we found that certain wraps were all one stem short. If you are getting only 19 stems in each wrap of red roses at Valentines instead of the full 20, this can represent a significant financial loss. Whenever we challenged a supplier about shortages they would claim that it was the automated machinery they used which was at fault. This might sometimes be true but occasionally we suspected that shortages were not accidental. It was very rare indeed to ever find a wrap with one too many stems in it!

We realised that our florists hated conditioning work and so we employed a Saturday girl to process the big delivery we received early each Saturday morning. We also hired a driver who could do conditioning work when not actually out delivering. The problem with this was that drivers didn't feel hugely motivated to do this sort of work. They were unlikely to hurry back to the shop after their last delivery of the day if they knew that conditioning work was waiting for them.

My complete lack of floristry skills meant that conditioning was just about the only task I could fulfil that involved handling flowers. Actually, I quite enjoyed conditioning early on a Saturday morning while chatting to Liz as she got on with the creative work. This may be a poor reflection on my intellectual

112

capabilities but I think conditioning is a bit like painting walls at home. It is very boring, but sometimes it is nice to do a job that allows you to think about something completely different to the task in hand.

Cut stems on the slant so that the largest possible area is able to take up water. If possible cut stems under water to remove airlocks which can occur during the time the flowers are out of water. Alternatively, try the new Oasis product! Strip off the bottom leaves to avoid decay and the build-up of bacteria.

If you have time, flowers with hollow stems should be turned upside down and the stems filled with water using a narrow spout. The stem ends can be plugged with cotton wool which acts as a wick to draw water up the stem.

Some stems contain a milky fluid and they should be cut and singed with a flame. Note that this fluid is an irritant to skin so avoid it touching your face or eyes. If this fluid should come into contact with the eyes then rinse well with cold water and seek medical advice.

Most mature foliage will benefit from being submerged for a minimum of two hours and then placed in a bucket of clean water and stored in a cool place for some 24 hours before using. If foliage is dusty and dirty a quick swish round in warm water with a little washing-up liquid, followed by a rinse in clear water will soon freshen it up.

Woody stems, young foliage and also roses can be revived by immersing in a couple of inches of boiling water for approximately 30 seconds. Cover the flower heads with a cloth to avoid steam damage and then immediately place in deep clean water for a minimum of 2 hours to remove air locks.

Narcissus contains a sap that, if mixed with other flowers, will shorten their life. Rinse the stems under running water to remove some of the slime. If you need to transport them with other flowers place them in a separate container within the bucket – a cut off plastic drinks bottle will do the job.

Tulips continue to grow so their stems often twist and turn, which adds to their individuality and beauty. Leave them wrapped in paper to keep them closed until you need to use them. A teaspoon of sugar in the conditioning water will help them. Some people prick under the heads to avoid the twisting but this is time consuming.

Violets can be floated on water as they take up water through their petals as well as their stems.

One of the best investments we ever made was to have a Chrysal dosing unit plumbed in. This meant we could use a separate tap to deliver a consistent measured dosage of preservative into each bucket or vase. We believed that this extended the vase life of most stock by some two to three days.

Establish a routine for getting all the menial, but still important, jobs done on a regular basis. These include changing the water in all the vases and buckets, watering plants and ensuring everything is priced. Check that there is no old stock slowly rotting away in a corner of your cold room. Not only will this stink but it also gives off ethylene gas that can harm the stock in the immediate vicinity. Most florists know that this gas also emanates from various types of fruit and it is a real problem for greengrocers who sell both fruit and flowers.

The ideal temperature for a cold room is generally reckoned to be between 4 to 7 degrees C. Often a cold room without full cladding, or with an underpowered chiller unit, will not be able to get down to these levels. However, as long as it keeps the temperature well below that in the shop it will still be a big help in prolonging flower life.

Wastage of stock

Stock that is deemed to be of poor quality once it is unwrapped should be put aside. Inform the supplier and either have the stock replaced, if the supplier is still in the locality, or have a credit applied to their next invoice. As long as you can demonstrate that the stock was not of merchantable quality then you should never have a problem in obtaining a credit. If you do, then you probably won't want to continue using that particular supplier unless you absolutely have to.

We found that in the early days of using a new supplier they would want us to keep any problematic stock. They would want to see for themselves that our complaints really were justified. Once suppliers realised that all our complaints were fair and reasonable their trust in us increased and then they told us not to bother keeping anything for inspection.

We kept a wastage log for anything we could not use. In this we would record all the details – the date bought, details of the stock and the supplier, the reason it was unusable and finally any action taken by the supplier. If it was simply stock that we had failed to sell within a reasonable timescale, this was obviously our problem.

When I first entered the floristry trade I assumed that wastage would be very high but I was pleased to discover that, with good organisation, this wasn't the case. Stock rotation is obviously essential and staff should use the oldest stock first. When new stock arrives, it can be very tempting for florists to pick the very best flowers for whatever they happen to be making. This has to be resisted and a very strict rotation system employed, with stock being used up while it still has a reasonable vase life left.

Open orders, when the customer leaves it up to the florist to select what they put into a bouquet, give you the opportunity to ensure that the older stock is used up while it is still of good enough quality. Many funeral orders also give the same opportunity to get your stock rotation right.

This really is a very important aspect of making retail floristry profitable. Letting staff use whatever they want can cost you an awful lot of money spread across a year.

We found that the Chrysal Professional 2 dosing unit significantly extended flower life as it very effectively delayed the flowers opening. Of course, every bouquet or bunch of flowers leaving the shop had flower food attached. This is essential in furthering the potential life of flowers once they have opened.

Mark-ups and pricing

As previously mentioned the mark-up you apply to the stock purchased is crucially important to your profitability. I have already explained that the usual method for cut flower pricing is to take the wholesale price net of VAT and to at least treble it to arrive at a retail price inclusive of VAT. Thus when the VAT implications are calculated this represents a real mark-up of at least 2.50 and this will be further reduced by unavoidable wastage.

Ideally you should aim to treble the net cost of each stem but many florists find that this makes them uncompetitive and they have to lower their prices. London florists may find they have to go to a multiplier of four or more to cover their exceptionally high costs.

The order sheet for each and every order should have the flower content listed and costed in case of complaint. This is not always possible for very urgent orders, however. When a customer dashes in demanding instant service because his car is on a double yellow line outside you have to act accordingly.

Customers in a hurry are not impressed by a florist carefully selecting each and every stem, listing their prices and adding it all up. Sometimes a £25 gift wrap has to be produced in not much more than a minute or two. However, an experienced florist knows what £25 worth looks like and can quickly make something appropriate with the right content.

Relay service orders, however, should certainly be properly costed and detailed. A reputable relay service provider like Interflora will usually insist on this.

The value of the flowers included in each made-up product should never be revealed to the customer. Occasionally in the event of a complaint it may be necessary to reveal this to Trading Standards. Nevertheless, some customers expect that a £30 bouquet will have £30 worth of flowers in it. It can be very frustrating trying to explain the simple metrics of a business to someone with this sort of expectation.

A retail florist will need to calculate the different costs involved in making different products. The average time taken to make up a gift-wrapped bouquet, a hand-tied bouquet, a pedestal arrangement and funeral sprays will differ considerably. We calculated the labour cost of each type of order and drew up printed tables which were displayed on the walls of the workroom. When a florist picked up a new order they referred to the table for that type of product and cross referenced this against the price and then read off the value of the flower content they should use. It is very important to get these tables right as they have a huge impact on your bottom line.

The mark-up multiplier used may vary at peak periods. Around Valentine's Day you may decide that if you use the normal multiplier for red roses they will appear to be extortionately expensive. Florists are open to very close scrutiny by the media at such times. You can probably use a smaller multiplier because the greatly increased volume of sales will still enable you to make a good profit.

At peak times it is also a good idea to let customers know just why prices are higher than normal. I used to provide a pile of one-page handouts on the shop counter explaining why our prices were higher than normal in Valentine's week. It explained that at peak times all florists naturally need to buy huge volumes of flowers. Nearly all of this stock is bought at the Dutch auctions. As with all auctions, if they are attended by lots of people, all determined to buy in huge quantities, then the prices paid will be much higher than normal. It is not rocket science!

The hand-out also explained that the growers spend far more than normal to bring very large volumes of flowers to readiness just at that particular time of year. Some of them are spending in excess of £10,000 per day on heating their glasshouses in the approach to Valentine's week.

We also explained that the roses we were selling were typically long stemmed, top grade, Grand Prix roses that had been properly and carefully conditioned. Comments in the media about supermarkets selling a dozen red roses for less than £10 on Valentine's Day absolutely infuriated me. It is like asking a Jaguar dealer why the car in his showroom is priced at £50,000 when you know where you can get a new car for £10,000.

You need to prominently display the current prices of all your cut flowers, perhaps on a whiteboard or blackboard. A simple solution is to use the little blackboard picks in each vase or bucket. These enable you to state both the flower name and the price per stem. Many customers do not know the names of most flowers and may be embarrassed to ask. They like to look around and then state confidently what they want

.

Marking up non-floral products

Mark-ups for giftware and add-ons are often lower than for fresh flowers. Many wholesalers who supply pots and glassware already have a retail price sticker on each item. This is normally double the wholesale price.

Balloons that can be bought for around £1 will retail for £5 when filled with helium and attached to a bouquet.

Many florists refuse to sell sundries such as baskets, Oasis, wire, ribbon, cellophane, care cards and message cards. They assume that anyone wanting these items will be an amateur florist or a flower arranger and therefore effectively a competitor. Some florists do sell these items but only at a very high mark-up. Others take the view that they will cooperate with such customers for the fresh flower sales they might also make to them.

Some florists actively cooperate with local groups of flower arrangers and college floristry courses. They might even offer them a discount on both flowers and sundries. This is a decision best made by individual shop owners based on their local situation.

Local floristry clubs and colleges can be a source for the recruitment of trainee florists and people doing work experience, so it can be useful to maintain a good relationship to get the pick of the best prospects.

There is certainly a risk in selling cards and/or envelopes that carry your shop name or your relay service name. Many florists can tell stories relating to how this has backfired on them. A typical example is a complaint from the recipient of some flowers. When investigated, it turns out that only the message card had been bought from the shop. An amateur florist had actually been responsible for the flowers and their make-up.

Peak periods

Planning for peak periods is one of the most important tasks of the year. Most florist businesses will make the majority of their annual profits over Valentine's Day, Mother's Day and Christmas. Order too much stock and wastage can be enormous. Order too little and you suffer the frustration of turning customers away.

I can remember when our main deliveries of stock arrived in the run-up to Valentine's and Mother's Day. The whole of the shop – the cold room, the store rooms and the sheds to the rear of the shop – would all be jam packed with new stock. There were flowers, vases, buckets and baskets everywhere. This was the only time I ever saw Liz looking really nervous as she tried to envisage just how we would ever sell it all. She was always nervous that she had got her calculations wrong and had bought far too much.

Every time we got to the end of Valentine's Day and Mother's Day, however, the shop would be as empty as if we had been invaded by a plague of locusts. Despite Liz's fears that one day we would come unstuck it never happened. However, if we had ever woken up to six inches of snow on Valentine's Day then it probably would have been a disaster.

Liz would put lots of effort into planning the buying for these peak periods. Usually I did any work that related to numbers and admin but this was different. Before each peak I would see her surrounded by paperwork from her history files, tapping away on the calculator. She would examine the previous year's invoices in great detail. She studied stem counts, exactly what she had ordered and what she had paid for it.

After each peak period we would sit down for a debriefing and make copious notes that went into the history file. These covered what sold easily, what didn't, what labour we used, what worked well and what didn't. We found these peak history files absolutely invaluable. Although we never really felt like writing lots of notes directly after such an exhausting period, we forced ourselves to do it. We knew just how much we would regret it the following year if we didn't do a thorough job of documenting everything.

The assumption we worked on for Christmas and Mother's Day was that, in comparison with the previous year, the volume of trade would be up by whatever was the average increase for the current year to date. However, calculating Valentine's Day is much more complex than that.

So what assumptions can you make if you are taking over a new business and you don't have any historical data to help with your planning? I have gone back through the sales records for all the years that we owned a shop and calculated how big an increase we experienced in the peak period weeks, over and above an average week.

Valentine's Day was always our busiest time of the year. On average, the sales for the week leading up to it were 235 per cent more than for a normal week. Thus for every thousand pounds taken in an average week, this became £3,350 in the week before Valentine's Day.

Mother's Day was always the second busiest peak with sales up 145 per cent above the norm. Many florists find that flower buying for Mother's Day has actually decreased in recent years. This seems to be because of the many alternative gifts and treats that are now promoted.

A long gap between Valentine's Day and Mother's Day is generally considered to be good news. A lot of people who buy flowers for the first occasion will look for a different gift if the second occasion comes soon after.

We never found Christmas anything like as challenging as these two main peak periods and average sales, in the two weeks prior to the big day, would only be 63 per cent above average. The actual volume of trade on Valentine's Day will depend mostly upon the day of the week that the 14th. happens to fall on, and also upon the weather. For almost all florists, Valentine's Day falling on a weekend is bad news. If it falls on a Friday, sales could be up 10 per cent on the overall Valentine's average. However , if it falls on a Saturday sales can be down by 10-15 per cent.

Fortunately, by sheer good luck, we never experienced Valentine's falling on a Sunday. When it did one year we were in between selling one shop and buying another. Those florists who have experienced a Sunday Valentine's tell me it is awful. Orders that would usually be delivered to a recipient at their place of work will mostly be lost. For various reasons, which I'm sure you can guess at, if Valentine's falls on a weekend, many senders will not want a delivery to be made to the recipient's home address.

At a week-end many people will prefer to take their partner out for a meal or they will shop for an alternative gift. Some central London florists, who rely almost entirely on commuter trade, do not even open for Valentine's if it falls on a weekend. So Friday is considered to be the best possible day, perhaps because people know that they will be in for a difficult weekend if they forget to buy flowers!

The weather also has a big impact. A bright sunny day is much more likely to promote a feeling of well-being and generosity. A heavy snowfall can be disastrous as, quite apart from keeping many customers at home, the delivery process can become a nightmare. We always hoped for relatively mild nights at peak periods. We were concerned that all the excess stock we had to store in outside sheds would be prone to frost damage.

In summary, plan for the peak periods with the greatest of care and do make the effort to carefully document what happens each year because in the run up to the next peak you will be so pleased that you did.

Giving products away

Every shop will receive a regular stream of requests to donate flowers to all sorts of charitable events. These may be for local schools, clubs, societies, raffles or auctions and it is best to decide at an early stage what your policy is.

I found it very annoying when someone regularly asked us to donate something, especially if they had never bought anything from us and we knew they bought their flowers elsewhere. Consequently we decided we would donate only to people or organisations who were also customers of the shop.

One of our account customers was the BBC and every year they would ask us to donate something for their charity auction. We were always pleased to deliver a large basket arrangement to them. The fact that they would describe it on the radio, and publicise us when they auctioned it, was an added bonus.

Other local businesses, who were good account customers, would also ask for bouquets and arrangements. They would either offer them as a raffle prize or auction them at a charitable event and we were only too happy to supply these.

We would politely tell non-customers asking us for freebies why we were declining their request. We explained that we received so many similar requests that we had to find a way of keeping our giveaways at a manageable level and consequently we only gave donations to regular customers. I found that almost everyone felt this was a fair and reasonable approach. As for the few people who didn't, we felt no obligation to give them anything anyway.

Buying stock – checklist

- Evaluate all wholesaler options
- Check wholesaler prices with other florists
- Be cautious over volume discount deals
- Balance cost against quality and service levels
- Be wary of cooperative ventures
- Don't stint on conditioning work
- Check stem counts occasionally
- Always get credits for poor quality stock
- Keep a wastage log
- Consider buying a dosing unit
- Get your mark-ups right
- Be very strict on stock rotation
- Plan, plan and plan again for peak periods
- Document what happens at each and every peak
- Take careful account of the day of the week that Valentine's Day falls on
- Take account of the gap between Valentine's Day and Mother's Day
- Establish a policy for give-aways

7 Building and optimising a website

This chapter addresses:

- The need for an excellent website
- DIY vs using a specialist
- Getting found by the search engines
- Search engine optimisation
- Check your website over
- Choosing your keywords
- Mobile friendly websites
- Using other companies' names

Having a really strong presence on the internet is absolutely fundamental in this day and age. Even if you are someone who hates technology and despises the internet you cannot avoid it. If you honestly believe that you can build a healthy and prosperous floristry business without the help of having your own website then I'm afraid I have nothing to teach you!

Not only is a website absolutely essential but it must be easily found by anyone searching the internet. The average person now uses Google, or one of the alternative search engines, multiple times a day. I am writing this at 9am and so far today I have used Google to find the opening times of a nearby pub, looked up the meaning of the word 'elysium' (for my crossword) and checked the price of a holiday in Norfolk. By the end of the day I will have used it umpteen times for all sorts of things. Like most people it is fundamental to the way I live my life.

I love Google! I honestly believe it has massively enriched my life and life would be much the poorer without it. I feel that with the help of my good friend Google I can find anything. It is the most wonderful resource and it is FREE! I take the view that if there is a business out there which I can't find through Google then it is not worth finding.

The need for an excellent website

The need for a strong presence on the internet is patently obvious these days. Whilst sat in a busy airport departure lounge recently I looked around at my fellow passengers. Every single person, without exception, was using either a mobile phone, a tablet or a laptop. When any of these people want to find a floristry service they will use the internet.

The internet is the shop window for any business in today's world. It enables you to tell the world what you do, show your entire range of products and services, list your opening times, provide a map showing where you are, provide lots of good customer reviews and all manner of other useful information.

Although your physical business premises might only be open from 9am to 5pm Monday to Friday, through your website you can be open for business 24 hours a day, 365 days a year. You can take orders and payments while you are asleep, in the pub or on holiday. The growth in online business has been exponential for some years now and this trend will only build and accelerate in the future. It is not to be feared, it is to be embraced. It is a truly wonderful resource which has changed the world.

One easy option which many florists have used is to take advantage of a service offered by several of the relay organisations. I think I am right in saying that this was first introduced by Interflora. The idea was that any florist shop which was a member of Interflora could use a template which gave them their own basic website describing the services they offered and giving information on how to contact them. This linked in with the main Interflora website and made it easy for customers to either deal directly with that shop or to relay an order via Interflora.

Some businesses liked the fact that this was a first step into the world of E-commerce. It was free and it was easy to do. Other shops took the view that it was too closely linked to Interflora and they would like to have more control over their own customer base. Whilst being happy to use Interflora to relay any non-local orders they really wanted their customers to deal directly with them.

DIY vs. using a specialist

If you just happen to be a website designer then you will have little need to read this chapter because you can develop your own perfect website. If your partner or a close friend just happens to be a professional website designer then your problem is probably solved.

It is possible to learn the basic skills and use one of the many templates available on the internet to build a website from scratch. To do this you do need a range of both technical and design skills. Despite having worked in the IT profession for nearly thirty years I personally wouldn't even attempt to develop my own website because I have absolutely zero talent for design. I cannot draw, paint or do anything at all remotely creative or artistic.

I suppose it is possible that I could do it if I worked very closely with someone like my co-author Jenny. As well as being a superb florist she can make all sorts of beautiful things from a variety of materials. Possibly she could tell me exactly what to put where and between us we could cobble together an attractive and functional website. However, this isn't the route I would go down. Sometimes you need to spend some money on external services.

I would look for an experienced website designer who has already developed lots of excellent websites for a number of floristry businesses. I would want to look at lots of examples of their work and navigate my way around real websites they have already built for real florists. I would study the feedback from their clients on what they thought of the look, functionality and cost of the work done for them.

I have spent considerable time looking at what is available in the UK and there are two website design businesses that I particularly like the look of: floristPro and Florist Window.

Both these businesses have a proven track record of having successfully designed and built a number of websites tailored to the needs of various different floristry businesses. They offer a full range of services which include the optimisation and maintenance of their customer's sites. They even offer the facility of a built-in relay service so you can send and receive relay orders without using one of the traditional relay services.

These specialist providers don't use a standard template so that your website looks just like lots of others. They provide a bespoke design tailored exactly to the needs of your business. They will create a website which can be used by customers using either a desktop computer, a laptop, tablet or smartphone.

You can take online orders and payments, display your own products and prices and even have the facility to update your own website should you wish to do so. Your website will show all your products with images and descriptions and entice customers to also order add-ons such as champagne, wine, chocolates, balloons and teddies etc.

Your website will probably do a much better job of developing an order to its maximum potential than most florists will when they are face to face with a customer in a shop. You can use banner adverts to publicise what you are offering for the peak periods and also provide promotional discounts to help you attract customers.

floristPro firstly provide an online demonstration to show you just what is possible, and then if you sign up they provide a starter pack which outlines the information they need from you to start the development process. They set up the payment process which enables customers to buy online from you and you get to review the final site before it goes live.

A quick-start training guide is provided and they hold regular training seminars which are free to all their customers. They have a dedicated support team who can make changes for you or show you how to do it yourself.

At the time of writing this in March 2017 the floristPro charges (exclusive of VAT) are as follows:

- A one-off payment of £79.95 for the setup of your website.
- An annual fee of £49.95 for an SSL certificate which ensures the security of payments on your website.
- A monthly fee of £49.95 to cover website hosting, content changes, upgrades and updates and, crucially, unlimited support and advice.

I must stress that I have absolutely no link with floristPro and will not benefit financially in any way should you choose to use their services. I am simply impressed by their work and the fact that over 600 florists in the UK have used their services. You can look at a number of these websites at www.floristpro.co.uk

I was also impressed to learn that in the British Florist Association Industry awards in 2016 all three Website of the Year winners were floristPro customers!

Getting found by search engines

It is one thing to have a fantastic looking website but if customers have difficulty finding it then all the hard work and expense can be wasted. I have already declared my admiration for search engines but what exactly are they?

A search engine collects pages from the Web and stores them in a gigantic database. It indexes all this information and provides a mechanism for people to search through it.

There are many different search engines. The most recent assessment of how many searches are made in the United States, using which search engine, was as follows:

1. Google   65.4 percent
2. Microsoft (Bing)   19.7 percent
3. Yahoo   11.8 percent

There are other much smaller players like Ask and AOL, but given that Yahoo gets its search results from Bing there are really only two you need to consider. It is obvious that Google is the industry leader by a mile and you can see why the word google has become one of the most commonly used words in the English language. Every day I hear people say 'I must google that'.

Having spent most of my working life in IT I am massively impressed by Google's ability to store, cross reference and find the most gigantic amount of data – it is absolutely staggering. It is amazingly fast, incredibly efficient and free! Anyone can find just about anything in seconds if they ask the right questions.

When I teach people how to use the internet I like to set them some homework each week. I give them the Daily Telegraph general knowledge crossword and ask them to use Google to complete it. One lady in her eighties, who had never used the internet before, would proudly present me with the completed crossword a week later. All thanks to Google!

So you need to make sure that Google and Bing can find your business. The difference it will make can either make or break your business. All successful businesses invest a lot of time and money in making sure they can be easily found by as many prospective customers as possible. There are businesses out there who have grown their sales twentyfold through their astute use of the possibilities available in the modern world of E-commerce.

When you search for a business, the search engine will list various possible links which are provided for free, and also some paid-for ads. Often these ads are referred to as PPC ads (pay per click) – meaning that every time someone clicks on an ad the website owner is charged by the search engine provider. These PPC ads can generate extra business but they can also create problems. There have been many instances where a small business has been repeatedly clicked on many times by a rival, just to cost them money. Small minded but true!

I have heard of one florist who, every time they had a quiet moment, sat at their computer just repeatedly clicking on their rival shop around the corner! The likes of Google get very annoyed with the many claims for refunds from disgruntled website owners who have fallen victim to this.

Search engine optimisation

Search engine optimisation, or SEO as it is now commonly known, has become a key skill in the internet world. Many medium and large businesses employ Search Engine Optimisers and the difference they can make to their employer's bottom line can be enormous.

How Google and other search engines manage to find, evaluate and compare the trillions of website pages is not generally known. It is a closely guarded secret and it is a set of algorithms that are extremely complex and constantly changing. Google don't want you to know how they do it! If you somehow found the perfect solution today for getting your business to the top of the rankings it will probably have changed by tomorrow.

I have found that if you ask a website designer if they can optimise your website so that it appears prominently in the Google listings the answer is always yes. You have to be sceptical as to just how true this is. Ask for a list of florist businesses that they have developed sites for and then see how easy they are to find via Google.

There have been a number of cases where a small business has used a professional website design business and have then found that they rank very poorly in the Google listings despite having been told their designer was an SEO expert. On challenging them they have responded that further optimisation is chargeable separately from the actual design work.

I have been googling a random selection of florist websites created by both floristPro and Florist Window and the results are mixed. They rank reasonably well but like most shop sites they come below most of the newer mail-order operators who give the appearance of having a shop everywhere.

I randomly googled 'florists in Bradford' and top of the listings was one of these mail-order operators who appear to have created a page for just about every town and city in the country. The word 'Bradford' appeared 17 times on this page and the casual visitor would assume they did indeed have a shop in Bradford - and just about everywhere else too!

The main keys to getting your website found by the search engines are to very carefully use keywords and to get other websites to contain a link to yours. The keywords might seem obvious but there is more to it than most people think. If you have a florist shop called Busy Lizzy in Manchester then the keywords Busy Lizzy, Florist and Manchester are obviously crucially important. We will cover this subject in more detail in later topics within this chapter.

The search engines assume that if your website is really significant then there will be other websites containing a link to it. This link counting is very important and something you should give a lot of thought to. You can get links by using all sorts of services like local business directories and any business or social contacts you have, who are prepared to mention you in their website, or on whatever social media they use.

Check your website over

A little fine tuning can make a lot of difference to how well your website works with regard to the search engines. You certainly need to make sure that you are actually in a search engine or a directory.

As an example if your website is called www.busylizzy.co.uk then on the Google toolbar enter site:busylizzy.co.uk

Google will then display a list of the different pages it has found on your site and you can see which pages they are. It shows the number of results and the time it took to find them. At the end of the URL (Uniform Resource Locator – basically just an address of a web resource) for each page there is a little green down arrow. If you click on this and then click on 'Cached' Google will display the actual copy of the page it has stored in the cache. A cache is simply a temporary storage area in which the search engine places a copy of what it found the last time it downloaded that particular page.

This search process allows you to see just which of your website pages Google knows about. Bing also uses the little green down arrow and Yahoo puts a 'Cached' link in grey text at the end of the URL.

If you enter your website address in the Google search box and click on 'Search' Google will display the sites home page information at the top of the results, followed by more pages from within the site and also other sites which have a link pointing to your site.

So what do you do if you search for your website and the search engines can't find it? It could be there are no links from any other websites which point to your site. You can rectify this by pestering friends, relations and colleagues to link to it from their own sites, or from whatever social media accounts they may have.

You can submit your site to the search engines by submitting something called an XML sitemap and you should talk to your website designer about doing this.

Another reason the search engines can't find you may be because you purchased a domain name that has been blocked, perhaps because it was previously being used for some dodgy purpose. You can find out if your domain name has ever been used before by using a service at www.domainhistory.net

Search engine optimisation is getting more and more complex as the business world learns how crucially important it is to their sales. More and more people are learning the intricacies of SEO as they try to outdo each other. Unfortunately there is a firm belief in the industry that you shouldn't trust your website designer to get SEO right. As mentioned earlier they all claim they are experts on SEO and can handle it for you but in practice many of them either don't understand it well enough or they are unwilling to invest enough time in it.

When you pay someone to handle the design and construction of a website you can visibly see what it looks like and you can test how well it functions. The aspects relating to SEO are largely hidden and very difficult for a layman to check out.

If your competitors are ranking more prominently than you, this is usually because they have done a better job at creating links. Get your website designer to do a link analysis on them to see how many links they have, which keywords are used in these links and what types of websites they are receiving links from.

The search engines look at text rather than pictures so you can perform poorly if you have lots of beautiful pictures of flowers and fancy graphics but very little text. You really need a lot of text content – the more words you have the more frequently your keywords can appear. It may seem cool to have lots of multimedia but the search engines are not overly impressed by it. The mega successful sites such as Amazon tend to focus much more on lots of text detail.

So the key things to focus on are getting your keywords right and getting the absolute maximum number of links from other websites.

Choosing your keywords

We have already looked at the sort of obvious keywords to use but this is an aspect that really requires a lot of thought. If you set up a Google account you can access a tool called Google Adwords Keyword Planner. You type a keyword into the search box which you think potential customers might use. If you then click on 'Get ideas' it will provide a list of keywords and how often they are used by people searching.

If you don't do this, perhaps because you are certain you know what words your customers will enter, you can make some seriously big mistakes. Some websites have been constructed to focus primarily on one particular word and the owner has subsequently found out that this word is in fact only third or fourth in the rankings.

It could be that your first choice turns out to be a winner – perhaps it is florist or flowers. You should also take account of commonly used misspellings – people who don't have English as their first language may type in florrist or flours so find ways to cover all your bases.

It makes a difference where your keywords are placed. The search engines use both the position and also the format as clues to the importance of words. Put keywords close to the tops of pages, into heading tags and bullet lists. Try to use keywords multiple times on a page but don't make it excessive or the search engine will figure this out. Use them in folder and file names and use them in bold and in italics.

Examine your site's access logs to see which keywords people have used when they have clicked on a link to your site. Talk to everyone you can about what words they would search on if they were looking for a business like yours.

Mobile friendly websites

There has been a huge growth in people accessing the internet from their smartphones and it is thought that this will soon exceed searches made from desktop computers, laptops and tablets. There was widespread panic in the SEO world when Google announced it will take into consideration how well a site displays on a mobile, when it receives a search request from such a device. So if your site doesn't display well it may fall in the rankings whenever someone tries to find you from their smartphone. Laptops and tablets shouldn't be affected but smartphone searches can be a problem.

If you are having a new site built, it is imperative that it should be developed as a mobile friendly site. There are now plenty of tools available, so this isn't too much of a problem. Having an existing site adapted might take quite a bit of work though.

Google's recommended method of adaptation is something called Responsive Design and it is probably the most used method at present. It uses HTML (the language used for website creation) to automatically modify the layout of a website's pages to suit whichever type of device is being used.

An alternative method is Dynamic Serving, which utilises two different versions of your website – one is for smartphones and the other for larger devices such as desktops, laptops and tablets. The server figures out which version to transmit when a particular page is requested.

It is worth noting that floristPro don't make any additional charge for their Mobile Responsive service, it is included as standard for their customers. Florist window provide a similar service for a charge of £20 per month.

Using other businesses names

A number of floristry businesses have found themselves in trouble for improperly using the name of a competitor or relay service on their website. Often this is in the hope that when people search on something like 'Interflora' their own business may show up in the Google listings. Some florists have illegally used relay service names and logos on their websites, stationery and delivery vans.

Although using a name like Interflora as a keyword may get a florist into hot water there are legitimate ways it could be included in the text of a website and would be taken account of by a search engine. As an example, I am sitting in Ipswich writing this and have just googled 'Interflora' – the search results show two florist shops in Ipswich. One of these is indeed a member of Interflora but the other isn't – they are a member of another relay service.

There is nothing to stop any business making references to other businesses on their websites and in their publicity material. For example, BMW might claim that one of their models has better fuel economy than the equivalent model in the Mercedes range. By the same token a florist might state 'we provide a relay service through eflorist, which is similar to that provided by Interflora'.

So it may be that you can get some traffic from people googling the name of your town and the word 'Interflora', even if you have no connection with Interflora, but you must do it carefully and legally.

When I was an Interflora member I would get very frustrated when people told me they had contacted another florist in Cambridge to enquire if they took Interflora orders and had then received a positive response. It is one thing for a non-Interflora shop to say 'no, but we provide a similar service using a different relay company' and quite another to simply say 'yes'. Unfortunately many shops do this but as I say, there are some sneaky, but legal, ways around this using the internet.

Since 2008 Interflora has been fighting a court battle with M&S over the use by M&S of the word 'Interflora' as a Google Adword on it's website. Interflora regarded this as a trademark infringement and M&S disagreed. Initially Interflora won the case in 2013 with the judge remarking that when members of the public typed Interflora into Google it did not enable reasonably well-informed and reasonably observant internet users to tell that the flower delivery service offered by M&S did not originate from Interflora.

In 2014, however, the court upheld an appeal from M&S and stated there would have to be a retrial. At the time of writing this case has still not been resolved and so after nine years, and a huge amount of cost, the business world is still waiting for a definitive judgement on the legal use of Adwords.

I have studied many legal websites for clarification and it seems that the distinction is whether you are using it in a way that makes the customer think they are buying from the other company. So you cannot use the word Interflora (or any other relay service) in a way that implies you are part of the Interflora organisation. You can, however, 'use it in prose'.

Building and optimising a website – checklist

- What specialist help will you use?

- What should your website content be?

- How will your website be found?

- Can you afford 'pay per click'?

- How well does your website rank with the search engines?

- How well does your website compare with those of your competitors?

- Get the right balance of pictures and text

- Are your keywords right?

- What are your customers searching on?

- Is your website mobile friendly?

- Are you using other businesses names legally?

8 Effective use of Social Media

This chapter addresses:

- Why you should consider social media
- Facebook
- Twitter
- Instagram
- Using hashtags
- Writing a Blog
- Linkedin
- Snapchat
- Videos and YouTube
- Listening in on social media

Many people decry the use of social media and swear that they would never use the likes of Facebook or Twitter.
Unfortunately there is an awful lot of rubbish and pointless drivel being communicated but there are also many businesses profiting greatly from social media.

I must admit that when people tweet 'I was going to have shreddies for breakfast but decided to have toast' this does not add much to the richness of life. There are also many problems caused by information getting into the wrong hands. There are countless stories of people saying they only used it for a very small circle of friends and family but then the unexpected happened.

Don't let this put you off though, because many thousands of businesses are significantly growing their sales and profits through the effective and business-like use of social media.

Why you should consider the use of social media

When I first got involved with the world of floristry I found it very old fashioned. Coming from the world of I.T. I was amazed to meet many florists who avoided any form of computer like the plague. People told me they hated the internet and just didn't understand the world of PCs and iPads etc.

In recent years I have taught a number of business sessions at Judith Blacklock's school of floristry in Knightsbridge. On these courses I have met a new breed of talented young florists who are just as familiar with their tablets, smartphones and social media as anyone else.

Just recently there was an article in the Daily Telegraph headed 'Social media drives the boom in flowers'. This article states that there is a new generation of bright young florists who are ripping up the rule book. There are florists who have many thousands of followers on social media who avidly look at their 'floral imagery'. One florist featured in the article has 127,000 followers on Instagram and thanks to her social media presence she works on prestigious events around Europe.

For many of the new wave of designer florists their website and their social media presence has become their shop window. It is a window that is way more effective than any traditional florist shop window. Potential customers are looking for originality and they are doing it via their computers, tablets and smartphones.

The likelihood of success does depend largely on how artistic a florist is and how dedicated they are to keeping both their website and their social media presence interesting. Your followers are looking for something new and different, although some of the new trends are actually a return to some quite traditional floristry of yesteryear.

People use social media because they want to communicate and share information quickly. With a basic website customers look at the site, read about the services and products that are offered and may then make a purchase. It is all one-way. Using a social networking service gives the opportunity for multi-channel communication – members of this new community can communicate with any other member who might want to communicate with them.

There are now well over a billion people using social media every day and it has become an amazingly effective way for people to find others with similar interests and to share messages, information and pictures.

These social-networking sites have made publishing easy to do for even those with no technical I.T. skills. Instead of just finding and reading information on the internet just about anyone can now become an online publisher.

Social media for businesses is at its most effective in sectors where there are a huge number of potential customers. Using it for a manufacturer of turbines for power stations probably wouldn't make much sense, but for an industry like floristry, where there are many millions of potential customers, it can be a real boon.

It is possible to get carried away with social media however as so many people find it so much fun. You don't want be glued to your tablet when a customer phones demanding to know where that hand-tied is that you should have delivered an hour ago!

Some retail sites have hundreds of thousands of followers and they use social media extensively to publicise new products and offer various discounts. Social media can be an incredibly effective way to put your business in front of the general public and showcase just what you have to offer. The old traditional florist shop largely relied just on people looking in their window but the world is a very different place now.

Facebook

With way over a billion users Facebook is the clear number one of the social media world. The type of businesses that do well on Facebook are those with attractive and interesting products and services to sell and consequently it is eminently well suited to the world of floristry.

There are many floristry businesses that have a large part of their customer base following them on Facebook. People who want to know what is new with their favourite florist.

It is very easy to put your business on Facebook because there are lots of free 'how to' guides on the internet. You can start by setting up your personal page and then create a business page. Use your business logo as your profile photo. Your cover photo should communicate why people like your products and services, so use a particularly impressive flowery picture. You could use a picture of your very smart, uniformly dressed delivery driver handing over a fabulous hand-tied to a delighted customer.

In the description sections show your services, products, address, opening times, contact details, positive postings from visitors, reviews, news items and upcoming events.

Take a lot of care over writing a concise summary of what your business does in the 'About' section. This is where you should really stress the benefits of what it is you do and why you are different from other florists.

Your description might be 'For over thirty years Susan's Flowers has provided beautiful floristry for every type of occasion and has established an unrivalled reputation for style and value.'

Your profile pages on Facebook are your shop window and need to be as complete as possible. You can greatly increase the chances of people wanting to interact with you and they also give Google more content to index, which will improve your chances of doing well when people search for the sort of services you offer.

You should think of your Facebook posts as a magazine. Don't just show products and discount deals but get the reader interested with articles and news items which are regularly updated and added to. Statistics show that Facebook business pages that are crammed full of advertising don't work nearly as well as those that have a broader balance of the necessary commercial stuff and really interesting content.

Twitter

Twitter is widely regarded as being second only to Facebook in its appeal and usefulness. It provides the ability to send short messages (of up to 140 characters) to the world at large. It is fast and easy to read so you can track hundreds of individuals and businesses who you find interesting.

Twitter is free to use and you can 'follow' people you find interesting and 'unfollow' if you decide someone has ceased to be interesting to you. It must be admitted that there is a huge amount of drivel on Twitter – messages which it is hard to see why anyone would be remotely interested in reading them. However, this shouldn't blind you to the fact that a huge number of business are using it to tell both customers and potential customers about newsworthy things they have to say.

Most users of Twitter quickly decide upon whether you are sending out worthwhile messages or drivel and will then make a sensible decision on whether to follow you or not. When people read a tweet (a Twitter message) they consider to be interesting, and of use to their contacts, they can 'retweet' it and consequently it is possible for something to very quickly go viral. This can be a wonderfully effective way for a business to quickly get a promotional message to a lot of potential customers.

Unfortunately just as Twitter can rapidly spread a positive message it can also quickly spread a negative message and sometimes with dire consequences. One well publicised example occurred when Waitrose tweeted customers asking them to complete the sentence 'I shop at Waitrose because…' One recipient responded with 'I shop at Waitrose because I like to feel important and I hate mixing with poor people.' A lot of people found this amusing and it was widely retweeted but it certainly wasn't the sort of response Waitrose were hoping for.

Instagram

Instagram is the most widely used image-based social network with over 300 million regular users. Many billions of photos and videos have been published on Instagram and on an average day more than 70 million pieces of content are published. It is mostly used by young people with disposable income and is consequently thought to be ideal for florists.

There are a huge number of florists using Instagram to show beautiful images of their floral creations. Instagram users like to view trendy and visually appealing pictures and are typically not interested in pictures of business premises etc.

Instagram is a mobile app aimed at the smartphone and tablet user. You can download on to iOS and Android platforms and also to Windows Phone 8 and later. It is very different to the likes of Facebook and Twitter in that you can't post links within Instagram posts. The only clickable link is in the 'About me' section of your profile page.

Using hashtags

Within social media you can use Hashtags to link up to new audiences for your images and products. You might write a post including #handtied which will have the effect of linking your posting with others that relate to handtied bouquets. Anyone searching on #handtied will be linked with lots of postings by florists and lots of links to click on their websites.

Hashtags are very important on Twitter because they give people the opportunity to take part in conversations on things that are of interest to them. Including a word in a tweet that is preceded by # makes it a clickable Hashtag. Anyone clicking on that particular Hashtag can view all the other tweets that use that same Hashtag.

Similarly you might also use #flowers for lots of similar links but something like #giftwrap isn't specific enough for a florist – it will link you with masses of images of gift packaging and wrapping materials. You can use the search feature to find Hashtags and there are many of them. The single most popular Hashtag is #love.

Instagram allows you to upload a maximum of 30 Hashtags per post so this gives you 30 opportunities. It is worth experimenting with different Hashtags. I have just searched on #interflora and predictably found lots of links to Interflora's website. But if someone was searching generally for any relay service they might search on #relayflowerservice – I have just done that and interestingly it took me to just one website, a florist shop in Bath. So with a little background work it is possible to be quite creative in finding different ways to entice people to look at your business.

Hashtags should be seamlessly integrated into a tweet, eg.
'Some of the most beautiful #handtieds are made by #Jennifleurs florist shop in #Colchester.'

Writing a Blog

The focal point for all your social media activity will typically be your blog (also called a weblog). This is a journal, or diary, usually written in an informal conversational style. It is where you write about all the new and interesting things happening in your business, publish ideas, create opportunities for communication and strengthen your websites ranking with the search engines.

The problem most people have with a blog is keeping it up to date. So many people are hugely enthusiastic when they first set it up and they add to it every day but over time this enthusiasm often wanes. Once a frequent visitor starts to find that it hasn't been updated, since the last time they looked at it, they will quickly lose interest.

To maintain a blog you must have plenty of self-discipline. It can be difficult to motivate yourself to do this at peak periods like Valentine's, but this is when your followers are most likely to visit. It can be difficult to apply yourself for half an hour when you are on holiday but you have to find something new, different, but still relevant to your floristry business to write about. If you think you are unlikely to keep it regularly updated then it is best not to even start.

Most people who write a blog worry about their customers and peers not liking it. If they make mistakes they worry about their credibility and the possibility of losing face. In practice your early postings will be read by very few people and so you do have time to settle into becoming more proficient. Like everything in this chapter there is lots of free advice on the internet about just how to set up and maintain a blog.

You must think about who you are writing it for and what they can get from it that will make it worth their time reading. You must show them how you provide solutions to their needs and casually mention your products and services in a very natural way.

Your blog can be built into your website and have the same look and feel as all the other content. It may be best to get your website creator to look after the graphics and the layout to create the right sort of professional image.

You should plan the content very carefully so that the typical questions your customer base has are regularly answered in differing conversational ways. Find ways to get the message across about all your specialist services for contract work, weddings, funerals and events etc.

Use pictures and videos in your blog to make them more interesting and to increase the time visitors spend on your page. Posts with pictures are sure to get more visibility on Facebook so try to use a really eye-catching image.

Linkedin

Linkedin is very much aimed at the business world and is probably the preferred social network for most professionals. Over 400 million people use Linkedin and nearly 3 million businesses have their own Linkedin page.

It tends to be used mostly for business-to-business communication but can also be used for business-to-customer. It uses a business profile page, much like Facebook, and is heavily used for recruitment – many businesses will look at an applicant on Linkedin before reading their CV. Because it is used mainly for B2B (business to business) the tone of the posts are mostly more professional and business-like than on other social media. Don't expect to get the same sort of sharing and liking activity that you may be used to on something like Facebook.

Don't ignore Linkedin just because you are dealing mostly with the general public though. There is much lucrative and regular work to be had for a florist in winning contract work for businesses and these customers are likely to be impressed if you are on Linkedin.

Snapchat

Snapchat is quite different to other social networks but is hugely popular with younger people. Basically it is an app that lets people send each other pictures and videos that disappear after ten seconds. It initially became popular amongst people who were 'sexting' and didn't want the images they sent to be recorded by anybody. It then became evident that Snapchat were actually retaining all images and they offered a chargeable replay service. Consequently a lot of the perceived security benefits lost weight.

Although the majority of Snapchat users are young and female, men are still sending some 400 million images a day via Snapchat. It is heavily used by businesses to promote new products and special promotions. It can be a good way to showcase new floral products to your customers and to send reminders about Valentines and Mother's Day.

As a busy florist you may feel that there is only so much time you should dedicate to social media and it is probably best to develop a strategy that enables you to keep your presence up to date on just the major platforms. Talk to your website provider about perhaps setting you up on Facebook, Twitter and Instagram and, if you have time, consider an online blog.

Videos and YouTube

YouTube has become the largest online library of videos with over a billion users watching some 4 billion videos every day. It is owned by Google and for most purposes it is free to either watch or upload videos on to the YouTube platform.

Users can search on whatever interests them and select an appropriate video to watch. As an example, I have just searched on 'making a handtied bouquet' and there are lots of videos to choose from, made by florists all over the world. They have been watched by many thousands of people and the most widely viewed video on hand-ties has so far been watched 822,000 times. It was made by an American florist and she uses the opportunity to showcase her business in the best possible light.

There are a huge number of flower related videos out there and a huge audience that watches them on a regular basis. When you consider that this sort of service is free it has to compare very favourably with the old fashioned, and often expensive, adverts in the print media.

You can 'watermark' your video with the name of your website and make yourself known to a huge audience. Try using a new and topical eye-catching name such as 'Making the 2018 Mothers Day bouquet.'

You can, of course, include similar videos within your website but don't overdo it. Contrary to popular belief many SEO (search engine optimisation) experts suggest that videos don't help your search engine rankings very much.

Listening in on social media

Most of the effort you put into social media concentrates on talking and getting your messages out there, but listening is important too. Obviously you will be interested in anything which relates directly to your business but you should also take a wider view.

Check out content posted by your competitors and stuff that relates to the floristry world in general. There is a gigantic amount of useful information on social media about flowers, trends, opportunities and every aspect of the modern world of retail floristry.

Even listening out for complaints can be beneficial. Some florists have picked up on a local customer who is unhappy about the product or service from one of their competitors and they have jumped in with a special offer to steal the business. I don't think I would recommend this approach as you can make some serious enemies this way, but be aware that you could be on the receiving end of this sort of opportunism.

More constructively you can use social media to turn a problem into an opportunity in a positive way. If you know that you have screwed up, then go out of your way to put things right. Do more than the customer is expecting and publicise it. If you have made a really big mistake then deliver a replacement product AND give the customer a full refund. There are many examples of this sort of action resulting in a disgruntled customer becoming one of your biggest fans and then telling the world how brilliant you were at fixing their problem.

Finally, don't let any personal prejudice about social media stop you from understanding that the world is changing fast and not using SM in the floristry trade of today can cost you an awful lot of business.

Effective use of Social Media – checklist

- Realise the importance of social media to business today, even if you hate the likes of Twitter!
- Take a structured approach to link your social media presence with your website
- Use Facebook as another shop window
- Be careful when soliciting responses from customers on Twitter
- Be aware of how complaints can spread across social media
- Don't start a blog unless you are 100 per cent committed to keeping it up to date and interesting
- Consider using Linkedin for communicating with business customers
- Consider Instagram for showcasing your latest creations
- Use social media to listen in to the rest of the floristry world
- Keep tabs on your competitors through SM

9 Operating expenses

This chapter addresses:

- Rent and leases
- Business rates and refuse disposal
- Water rates
- Heat and light
- I.T. and communications
- Insurance
- Finance charges
- Delivery vehicles
- Maintenance and repairs
- Avoiding scams

There are many elements of a businesses operating expenses, such as rent, water, heat and light, business rates and wages which are unavoidable. Some of these will be costs you can't change or avoid but you do have a choice over just which supplier you will use. Some costs, such as advertising, are optional and you choose how much to spend or indeed, whether to spend anything at all.

Every business is pestered almost daily by people trying to convince you that they have a service, or product, that is perfect for you. Usually they don't and talking to them is a waste of valuable time which would be better used for profitable purposes. These calls can be very annoying and you should develop techniques for cutting them short and dissuading them from calling again.

Unfortunately these days most cold callers are not put off by a polite refusal and you usually have to be extremely blunt to cut them short and get them off the line.

Rent and leases

Having negotiated the rent at the beginning of a lease there is usually very little you can do to change it until either the next rent review is due, or the current lease is up for renewal. At the time of taking out a lease you should know just what you are committing to.

As mentioned in an earlier chapter, most leases are classed as 'repairing leases', meaning you are responsible for maintaining the property in a good condition and for any repairs and renewals that are necessary. You should try to get the landlord to accept as much responsibility as you possibly can and to take account of the condition of the property. Don't get into a position where you are liable for huge bills for subsidence, damp or rot which has been present for perhaps many years.

Either have a professional survey done before signing the lease or at least take lots of photos of all the weak points. One of the biggest bones of contention is often the condition of window frames and surrounds, so take lots of close up pictures which you could use to contest unfair charges in the future.

It is common practice for a lease to contain a clause stating when the rent will next be reviewed and this also needs negotiating. Often the small print of the lease will state that at the review the rent can only be reviewed upwards. This should be fiercely contested, because if the general economy hits hard times and adjacent premises are empty, you have a good case for the rent being reduced.

You will usually want the review to be as far into the duration of the lease as possible. If your landlord asks for what you deem to be an unreasonable increase you should employ the services of a surveyor. They will assess the current market rate for similar premises in the area and negotiate accordingly.

Before employing a surveyor, you should examine how they intend to charge for the work they do. It is quite common for the surveyor's fee to be a percentage of the agreed rent negotiated. I think this is absolutely bizarre and wrong because it means the higher the agreed rent, the higher the surveyor's bill will be. Basically, using this method, you are rewarding the surveyor for doing a bad job. Some surveyors will tell you that is simply the normal practice but you don't have to agree to it.

When our rent review was due on the Cambridge shop I employed a surveyor and agreed a completely different method of charging. I worked out a scale of charges which rewarded him for driving the rent down to the lowest level he could possibly achieve.

The Royal Institute of Chartered Surveyors offers a special scheme for 'Rent reviews for small businesses' which includes a fixed scale of reasonable charges. Never assume that any scale of charges is non-negotiable though.

Business rates and refuse disposal

Business rates are levied by your local authority and the rateable value will relate to the size and location of the premises. It is well worth checking that the square footage figures they are working to are correct. It is also a good idea to chat to the proprietors of neighbouring shops to compare notes. If you feel you are paying too much then lodge an appeal.

The latest revaluation of rateable values has seen some alarming differences for different businesses in different areas. Some have seen their rateable value decrease while some have seen a 300% increase. It is certain that many businesses will want to challenge their new assessment and you can do this yourself on the gov.uk website.

There are many people who offer a service to get your rates reduced for you. These usually operate on a 'no win – no fee' basis and an experienced firm using qualified surveyors can win significant savings. Unfortunately there are a lot of sharp operators offering this type of service so it is essential to check them out and study the small print very carefully. Using a search engine can usually enable you to find out if anyone has had a bad experience of whoever you are considering.

Following the 2010 assessment of rateable values there have been, a quite incredible, two million appeals, of which 29 per cent have been successful. Using a professional RICS surveyor will definitely increase your chances of success. One firm are claiming that they have acted on behalf of over 20,000 businesses and achieved a success rate of 93 per cent. The fee they charge varies between 10 and 30 per cent of the amount saved.

It is normal practice to be charged separately by your local authority for refuse collection. The scale of charges will relate to the number and size of your bins so make sure you have the right capacity for your business. I found that the best approach was to pay for whatever bin capacity you would need for a typical week's business.

We found that it definitely helped to be on good terms with the bin men and we always gave them a generous tip at Christmas. There were occasional busy days when we simply forgot to put the bins out at the right time and the bin men would always put their head in the door and remind us. If sometimes we had a small amount of overflow rubbish they wouldn't complain.

At peak times like Christmas, Valentine's Day and Mother's Day, when we had lots of overspill rubbish, the friendly relationship always helped us. Taking your own refuse to the local tip can be very expensive. My local council is currently charging £54 for a van load of rubbish. You can see why many florists take their excess rubbish to the dump by car and pretend it is household rubbish. We found that giving the bin men an

156

occasional £5 tip was much more cost effective. In some areas there are alternative services to those provided by, or through, the local authority so it is worth shopping around.

Water rates

The main thing to check here is whether it is most cost effective to pay a fixed scale charge (if possible) or to have your supply metered, assuming you have a choice. Most premises are metered these days and you may have no choice but to simply pay for what you use.

Since April, 2017 business customers (unlike residential customers) in many areas have been able to choose which water supplier they use. Thus the sort of choice available for gas and electric supplies for many years will finally be available for water and sewerage supplies. So check out what options exist in your locality and shop around.

You should also seek to get your charges reduced, if you possibly can, for multiple meters or for interrupted service. Our Cambridge shop occupied what had once been three adjacent terraced houses. There were two different points for the water supply and consequently we received two quite separate invoices for water and sewerage. One of these supply points serviced the workroom, where we used considerable volumes of water, so we were happy to pay a fixed scale charge for this. The other serviced a part of the shop where there was just one tap and a second toilet and so we had that metered.

When we had occupied the Cambridge shop for a couple of years the local Water Board undertook some major work to renew the water main in a nearby road. This necessitated the closure of one lane of the road outside the shop. I took the view that this was disruptive to our business and was causing us significant loss of trade. A claims assessor worked on behalf of

157

us, and also other neighbouring businesses, to seek compensation.

To enable the assessor to submit a strong case I provided a lot of detailed accounting information to demonstrate how much our sales had dipped over the period of the disruption. It was a lot of work but I produced a detailed and verifiable spreadsheet containing all the data. It was all well worthwhile when we received a considerable cheque for the full amount claimed. Also the assessor's costs were met by the Water Board.

I subsequently found out that a number of neighbouring businesses decided it would be too much work to submit the same sort of business case that I put together and consequently they received nothing. You have to be prepared to put in some effort and I have found that when people see you have done a lot of detailed work they are much less inclined to argue the case with you.

Heat and light

Now that there are so many choices for where you get your gas, electric and perhaps oil supplies it is well worth shopping around. It is very easy to use the online switching services but be wary of some of the huge estimates they use for potential savings.

The switching sites make their money from commission and consequently it is in their interest to try to persuade you to change supplier, no matter who you may currently be with. They will show potential savings of many hundreds of pounds but these can be quite misleading and unachievable. There are many instances of someone changing to a new supplier only to find out days later that they have raised their prices, so it is usually best to change to a fixed term deal.

Changing supplier is often a lot of hassle despite what the industry claims and the switchover process can often result in some dual billing until you finally get things resolved. I must say it has improved in recent years though, largely because of government pressure on suppliers.

I have found that if you pick the best online deal, send your own meter readings and opt to pay by direct debit with paperless billing, then there isn't much difference between most suppliers. Of course, if you stick with the same supplier on their standard tariff, receive paper bills and pay by cheque then you will be massively overpaying.

It is well worth checking that you really are only paying for the gas and electric that you use. Often shops have flats above and it is not unknown for a shop proprietor to unwittingly be paying the bill for the flat above in addition to their own. We had multiple electricity meters in our shop which also covered three flats above. I labelled each of them and always checked that our bills were correct. You can't rely on the resident of a flat to tell you that they don't appear to be paying for their electric!

I.T. and telecommunications

As with heat and light there are many options for just who supplies you with your comms. With multiple phone lines, broadband and mobiles you have to carefully shop around for the best deal to suit your needs.

Usually an all-inclusive deal with a single supplier will give you the lowest overall cost but not always, so shop around. In the modern world good broadband speeds are essential to get you fast response times for multiple desk-top computers, tablets and smartphones.

Most of the different comms suppliers are actually using the physical BT network which still consists of an awful lot of copper wire. The likes of Virgin offer more modern and much faster fibre optic cabling but BT are catching up with them as they progressively roll out more new cabling.

It is likely that you will have some fixed monthly costs for software products and services. You may be paying some £50 per month to the supplier of your website to cover ongoing support and maintenance. If you are using a reputable supplier then I would suggest that for most people this is money well spent. It will be covered many times over by the increased sales that a well-constructed and optimised website will win you.

If you have considerable expertise and experience in I.T. you might be able to do this work yourself but the vast majority of people can't. Even though I have the best part of thirty years I.T. experience I would always use a professional website design business because I have absolutely no artistic flair and could never make my website look attractive.

You will probably also have regular monthly costs for an online accounting system. Products like Sage and QuickBooks enable most people to have an easy-to-use solution for just about all their book-keeping needs. For circa £25 per month you can have a system which gives you a complete solution for payroll, VAT, invoicing and final accounts. It will give you a profit and loss statement and a balance sheet at the click of a mouse. Once set up, the quarterly VAT return is simply a couple of clicks of a mouse. I still hear florists say they spent all day Sunday producing their VAT return – madness! Nobody should be doing this manually in today's world.

I believe that most small businesses can save almost all of the cost of a traditional accountant's services. The software and the user guides and books like 'Bookkeeping for Dummies' make this possible for the majority of people today. If you are totally conversant with using tablets and smartphones, and are prepared to do a little studying, you can probably handle your own accounting today.

Once you become conversant with modern bookkeeping software you will find that you have much more up-to-date information about your business than you would if you were making occasional use of an accountant. On any given day, you can generate a profit and loss statement for the last twelve months and use all sorts of reporting features which will tell you how all aspects of your business are performing.

If your telecom services are ever disrupted through no fault of your own then you should record all the details and seek compensation. One day we found that some of our phone lines were dead and spotted a man up a telegraph pole across the road. He said he was contractor working on behalf of a major telecoms supplier and they should have notified us of this planned work weeks before. I submitted a detailed claim showing our loss of business and this was duly settled in full – again, the more detail you provide the less likely it is to be disputed.

On another occasion BT made a mistake in implementing a new call divert system for us. They cut off our two main lines for more than a day and again we made a detailed claim which was settled in full. Don't seek just a rebate on your line costs – go for the full amount resulting from the loss of business.

There is one area of I.T. expenses where I would question whether saving money is really worth it. This is on cheap printer cartridges and refilled cartridges. I do a lot of printing and have experienced a number of problems with faulty cheap cartridges and refills containing short measures. I have had two instances of cheap cartridges actually damaging my printer.

I eventually decided that I would only buy new HP cartridges and avoid all the hassle. It is interesting that new HP printers are now checking the chip attached to each cartridge to see if it is a genuine HP cartridge. You should still shop around as the manufacturers prices vary from shop to shop but my advice is don't take chances with cheap cartridges.

Insurance

Search for the best deals for shop, buildings and van insurance. This does not necessarily mean finding the cheapest deal but the one which gives you the right balance of cost and cover. The companies that advertise in The Florist magazine are worth checking. They have identified florist businesses as a special vertical market and have put together tailored packages to meet the needs of the typical florist.

It is a legal requirement for any business employing one or more people to have employers liability insurance. This covers you for the costs associated with any claim from an employee over illness or injury due to their work. You can be fined up to £2,500 for each day without cover and you must display the appropriate notice of insurance to prove you have this cover.

You will need buildings and contents insurance, just as you have for your home. It is very unusual for a landlord to provide this cover and so it is usually the tennant's responsibility.

You should also seriously consider taking out business interruption insurance to cover you for any unforeseen disaster which prevents you from trading normally. Whilst buildings insurance will cover you for the material damage caused by fire or flood, the loss of income which ensues is often not covered.

Many small businesses have been forced to close down following a disaster as they could not survive without their normal sales income. So plan what would happen if you had to shut the doors for a period of weeks or even months.

Vehicle insurance for delivery vans can vary greatly depending upon the provider and the different drivers you need cover for. Drivers under the age of 25 can prove to be very expensive, as can anyone without a clean licence. Some insurers will place a limit on the number of different drivers you can have covered.

Most will charge an administration fee for any amendments you need to make as your workforce changes. A policy that guarantees you a replacement vehicle in the event of problems is well worth paying a little extra for.

Use the comparison sites on the internet but also try getting a quote from a broker as sometimes they can surprise with their best offers.

Finance charges

Most banks will offer small businesses free banking for a period, perhaps up to the first 18 months. After the initial free period bank charges can prove costly, so again you need to check the small print before opening a new account.

Examine the monthly statements to see how you can keep the charges down to a minimum. You should certainly be using online banking to keep the transaction charges down. Avoid using cheques wherever possible and make payment transfers online using BACS.

Ironically our bank in Cambridge implemented some hefty increases in their business account charges at the same time as they cancelled their regular weekly order for flowers. They told me they were very sorry but they just couldn't afford fresh flowers any more!

Every day I would log into the online banking system and examine what was in our different accounts. I shuffled money between accounts to take advantage of the small opportunities for earning a little interest. I would look at immediate outgoings that were due and ensure there was just enough in the current account.

Rather than paying cash receipts into the bank, I would use this money to pay visiting wholesalers to keep the associated charges down.

Changing banks can be a real nightmare. Even though most of them offer to make it as seamless and hassle free as possible there will always be lots of difficulties. You have to think of all your account customers who have your current account details in their systems. No matter how well you publicise the fact that you have changed banks you will still get lots of payments being made to the old account. Changing direct debits and standing orders is never straightforward in my experience. I think you have to be seriously fed up with your bank to make it worth the hassle of changing.

There are a range of different suppliers for the credit and debit card processing services you will need and their rates can differ greatly. In our first florist shop we were initially paying a service charge of over 3 per cent for credit card transactions. When we took over a larger shop we were able to take advantage of a deal, which Interflora negotiated for their members, which reduced these charges to a fraction over one per cent. When our card sales grew to well over £250,000 this made a big difference.

Delivery vehicles

When buying a new delivery vehicle, it is very nice if you have the cash to fund an outright purchase. It is very difficult to get a better deal than a well negotiated cash purchase. Some people will argue that you are better off entering into a leasing arrangement and investing your cash in some other aspect of the business but I would still advocate a cash purchase if you can afford it.

Instead of acquiring a traditional van it can be tempting to buy some sort of MPV (multi-purpose vehicle). This could be used mostly for deliveries with the seats down but also for ferrying the children around with the seats up. The problem is you can only reclaim the VAT on a van and not on a car. Also you should calculate the apportionment of business mileage and private mileage, as you can only reclaim the proportion used for business. This applies to all the costs relating to purchase, fuel, repairs and servicing. A van is defined by having no side windows behind the driver's cab.

Typically most delivery vehicles are diesel-engined, to take advantage of the better fuel economy. The combination of high mileage and better economy used to make this decision a no-brainer. The current trend of penalising diesel vehicles because of their emissions may change this justification in the future. The higher charges currently being proposed for congestion charges and parking charges in large cities means that petrol engines will probably become the preferred option for the future.

It can also make a difference what level of Euro-compliance a vehicle meets. At the time of writing this most new vehicles are Euro 6 compliant. There are new cleaner diesel vehicles which achieve Euro 6 and older petrol-engined vehicles that don't and so this also makes a difference to some of the new environmental charges being levied.

A lot of diesel-engine vans are incredibly reliable and achieve huge mileage – it is not unusual to see vans with several hundred thousand miles on the clock.

Paying for your fuel can be very easily managed with a fuel card for each driver. This way the drivers never need cash from the till for fuel. You receive a monthly VAT invoice that is best paid by direct debit. Also you can get regular reports showing what level of fuel consumption each driver achieves.

I know of one case where an employee always achieved much worse fuel economy than all of his counterparts. When his manager investigated this, he found that the drivers wife was in the habit of filling up her car at the same time, and on the same pump, as her husband was using for the van.

It is not unknown for a delivery driver to keep a spare fuel can in the van, which is always filled when the van is filled, and the contents are then transferred to a personal vehicle when nobody is looking. Unfortunately you have to be very vigilant.

Maintenance and repairs

If you, or perhaps your partner, are practical types who can handle most problems and repairs yourself then all well and good. It is as well that your staff know what to do in your absence whenever there is a problem.

Put a list of contact numbers up on the workroom wall showing your preferred builder, plumber and electrician etc. Also make sure the staff know how to contact your insurance company in the event of some unforeseen problem in your absence.

Once we were on holiday in the West Indies when somebody decided to drive around Cambridge on a Saturday night shooting at shop windows. As a result, we needed new glass in the main shop window and front door. This involved a great deal of hassle and many phone calls. We had to give Jo, the shop manager, and our son, the information they needed to check the insurance policy and take appropriate action. This taught me to make sure that all the insurance details were easily accessible from then on.

As our shop was an elderly property, with a lot of very suspect plumbing, I found it was always best to use the same plumber for any problems. He knew where all the stopcocks were and could quickly identify weak points in the pipework.

There were only two regular maintenance contracts that we entered into. One was for the refrigeration equipment in the cold room and the other was for the annual checking of the fire extinguishers. You must ensure you comply with all the health and safety requirements for signage and procedures.

The HSE (Health and Safety Executive) website tells you just how to develop a health and safety policy for your business, develop a risk assessment and provide the correct workplace facilities. It also shows how to make arrangements for first aid, health protection and dealing with accidents. You must also display the health and safety law poster.

You can bring someone in to do all this for you but, to save money, I would advocate studying the HSE website and simply following all their advice.

Avoiding scams

The level of attempted scams and con tricks is a major annoyance these days and they can waste an awful lot of time for both you and your staff.

Often our shop phone would ring and a voice stated that back in February they contacted us regarding advertising. They claimed that although you were too busy at the time, you allegedly promised that you would proceed later in the year. They would tell us that the advertising would be placed in a directory/diary/calendar. It would be aimed at benefitting the disabled/orphaned children/members of the emergency services/drug awareness etc.etc. Usually the truth is that you

167

never made them any promises and probably had never spoken to them before. The only person who would benefit from it is the person on the other end of the phone.

Another common scam is the one where the caller knows of someone who is about to register your business name as an internet domain name. This would enable them to steal lots of business from you. However, if you make an immediate payment to the caller they will get in first and register the name on your behalf. This is always a con as are the calls alleging to be from Microsoft or BT or whoever which can save you from imminent disaster.

There are a number of businesses that pretend to be the official Data Protection Registrar. They send you notification that you will be liable for prosecution unless you register with them immediately and send them a payment of over £100. The reality is that you do need to register if you are storing customer details but it only costs £35.

The annoying thing is that many of these organisations are not actually breaking the law as they will register your business if you pay their fee. They will claim that they were providing you with a service for which they are entitled to payment. The reality is you can easily do this yourself for a lot less money.

Phone calls and emails from people purporting to offer products relating to health and safety also imply that you have to spend money with them. They will say that whatever they are selling is mandatory to comply with current legislation. Always assume these are a con and seek advice from the official authority if you are unsure.

Credit and debit card cons are a constant problem and have continued to be after the introduction of chip and pin devices. One of the biggest problems for florists is orders placed over the phone. If the 'customer' is using someone else's card you will usually not know there is a problem until the dreaded charge-back from the card company arrives. A visit to the

168

recipient of the order will usually elicit the response that they have no idea who the sender is. Usually there will either be no name or a false name on the message card.

Often you can spot a dubious telephone order because it will be for an unusually high value. The caller will often want add-ons such as champagne and chocolates. Some of these callers are daft enough not to withhold their number and so dialling 1471 is always worth trying after a suspicious call. Always take a contact number from the caller and try to call back to confirm the order. If you get 'number unobtainable' you will know it's a con.

We had one caller who worked for a large department store in Cambridge and decided to send his Mum a large bouquet on Mother's Day. He paid for it using one of their customer's card details. The cardholder told me it was a new card which she had only ever used on one occasion. We worked very closely with the cardholder as we were both determined to nail the offender. Between us we were eventually successful in having him prosecuted. He was also fired by his employer and suffered the shame of his parents finding out exactly what he had done.

Any calls purporting to be from a bank or card company requesting any sort of financial details will almost certainly be bogus. A girl working in one florist shop took a call from someone claiming to be from the supplier of the shop's card processing services. They claimed they had suffered a major computer system failure which had resulted in all the card transactions that day having been lost. They said they could manually recover the situation if she relayed all the transactions to them over the phone. If you ever get a call like this put the phone down and try dialling 1471 before calling your card services provider and reporting the details.

Unfortunately contacting the police in the event of card fraud is usually a waste of time. No matter how much evidence you give them, they seem to treat it as low priority and cite low staffing numbers for their inability to investigate. It is also very

169

disappointing that the card companies often seem disinclined to take much interest. They often take the view that it is such a massive problem they don't have the manpower to investigate fraud relating to relatively small amounts of money. They hope you will accept a charge-back and put it down to experience.

I have always taken any fraud really personally and it makes me so mad that some low-life is attempting to make money out of my business. I have put a lot of time and effort into trying every avenue I could think of to track people down. Often when you put together all the detail you have relating to the order and to the recipient you can get a positive result. Probably I have sometimes spent more time than was profitable in chasing down these types of situation but I take it so personally I am absolutely determined to bring people to book. It is also very satisfying when you can get your money back.

Operating expenses – checklist

- Negotiate lease term, amount and all conditions
- Negotiate over the state of the property at commencement of lease
- Use an experienced surveyor for rent reviews
- Use an RICS surveyor to appeal against your business rates
- Check the square footage of your property for business rates purposes
- Shop around for the best supplier of water services
- Claim the full amount for any disruption to normal business caused by a utility provider
- Check that you are paying for only the correct gas and electric meters
- Be wary of the utility switching websites claims of amazing cost savings
- Be prepared to pay for ongoing website service and maintenance
- Use an online bookkeeping system
- Double check ALL insurance policies and costs
- Shop around for the best card processing services
- Compare vehicle leasing costs with outright purchase costs
- Be suspicious of EVERYONE trying to sell you ANYTHING!

10 Doing the books

This chapter addresses:

- The benefits of DIY accounting
- Drawing up budgets and targets
- The profit and loss statement
- Sales ledger
- Purchase ledger
- Payroll
- Accounting ratios
- Value Added Tax (VAT)
- Capital allowances
- Tax inspections and record keeping

Deciding whether you will attempt to do your own bookkeeping, or whether it is worth employing a qualified accountant to do it for you, is a big decision. It will depend largely on your own skills and your aptitude for the business side of things. If you have a basic knowledge of business fundamentals, and also some basic I.T. skills, then the sort of computerised accounting packages available today can make it very easy for you to do it yourself. This means you could be largely self-sufficient and keep much more up to date about just how your business is performing.

If you don't think you have the right skillset or aptitude then maybe you have a member of the family or a close friend who does. Unless you have really good accounting experience it is still a good idea to get ad hoc advice from an accountant. You must ensure that you are getting things right and complying with HMRC regulations. You might still need an accountant to check your work and draw up the final year-end accounts. It is very easy to miss opportunities for reducing your tax liabilities or to make errors in your year-end returns.

Before I got into the floristry world I worked for a large American computer manufacturer as head of their European education and training business. I had a string of offices across Europe, each with its own budgets and targets. My job was to deliver a profit from each and every country we operated in and convert everything into the right amount of US dollars to keep head office in Silicon Valley, California happy.

Every time I went to the U.S. my boss would say "Hi Alan, are you making your numbers?" Then he would enquire about my wife and kids. When I met the other heads of business units from around the world our first question was always "Are you making your numbers?"

I ate, slept and drank numbers. I felt I was always carrying a bunch of spreadsheets around in my head and figuring out how I could manipulate them to improve the bottom line. If your numbers were good you could pretty much do what you wanted. The bonuses were good, you flew business class, drove a very nice Mercedes, stayed in expensive hotels and ate in the best restaurants. If your numbers were bad life was miserable and you could be savagely beaten up and humiliated in the boardroom. I craved security and so learnt to always do whatever it took to stay on the right side of the equation.

The spreadsheets were like a sort of financial electrocardiogram and they certainly had a huge impact on your general health and wellbeing.

When I moved into the world of floristry I absolutely loved it. I took a massive cut in income but the joy of owning our own business made it so worthwhile. You can set your own budgets and targets and decide what to spend money on and what not to spend money on. You are the master of your own destiny and can choose how hard you want to work in the pursuit of your goals. You can choose to branch out in new directions and do radical things to change your business.

If you have set your business up as a limited company then you have to get your year-end accounts audited by an accountant.

These accounts will eventually have to be filed at Companies House. If you operate as a sole trader, or as a partnership, you can handle all the accounting yourself. But do so only if you are certain that you know what you are doing.

The benefits of DIY accounting

If you do feel confident about doing your own book-keeping there are so many benefits apart from the obvious cost savings of not employing a qualified accountant.

When we took over the Cambridge shop way back in 2000 I found that the previous owners had been spending over £2,000 a year on accountant's fees, yet the information provided was in my opinion minimal, very basic and always out of date. It complied with the needs of HMRC and ensured the staff were paid correctly but provided almost nothing in the way of management information.

If you do your own accounting it is easy to derive a whole mine of bang-up-to-date information about how your business is performing. You can examine sales trends and how well you are doing with the buying of stock. You can check that your staff costs are in line with your sales and whether all your different operating expenses are under control.

Every Sunday I would study the numbers relating to the past week's trading. We always wanted to beat the corresponding week from the year before and usually we did. If we didn't I would analyse the numbers to try to find the reason. Was the weather bad or did we get a poor deal on the stock we bought? Did we have some unusually big sales the year before? These are just some of the questions you should ask yourself.

I was frequently amazed when I asked other florists how things were at the moment and it became apparent they didn't really know. People would say 'I think Valentine's Day was quite good but I'm waiting for my accountant to tell me'. I find this amazing and a clear sign of a poorly run business. Modern accounting software will present you with a whole raft of invaluable detail right away.

Some florists only realise their gross margin has been slowly diminishing after a period of months or sometimes even years! Perhaps they have not been haggling well enough and wholesalers find them a soft touch. It could be that they are paying a fair price but the wastage has been increasing – and this might be because they have simply been buying too much. Maybe they are not cleaning buckets and vases well enough or perhaps because they haven't invested in a dosing unit.

If you rely on old-fashioned manual accounting then things like this can slide imperceptibly over a prolonged period of time. When you do finally find out you are too late to stop the net profit for the year slipping by several thousand pounds. You must detect problems quickly and then take prompt action to fix them.

Budgets and targets

When you make financial predictions for the future I always think a good dose of pessimism helps you to be realistic. Assume that there will be unforeseen problems and setbacks. When things do go wrong, as they always do at times for any business, you may still be able to achieve your targets and make an acceptable profit. I learned a lot from my time in I.T. that subsequently helped in our florist shops.

We all have the opportunity to learn lessons from history and from our own experiences in life – things we got right and things we got wrong. We can reflect on how we could have done things differently to avoid the problems. Past experiences will also help to mould your general approach and attitude to just how you run your business. I have certainly made masses of mistakes all through my life but I take the view that everyone else has too. The key thing is whether you face up to your shortcomings and do something about it. Arrogance in business is probably the most serious shortcoming of all.

When I worked in I.T. I built up a reputation for always beating my sales and profit targets but this wasn't because I was particularly clever. It was because I managed to tone down the wildly ambitious aims of our board of directors. Before each new financial year, I worked very hard to negotiate my targets down to realistic and achievable levels. I was frequently amazed that my American peers were so keen to please that they would agree to huge targets that were simply unachievable.

Having targets that are simply pie-in-the-sky are demotivating. Staff will give up on making the target as soon as the first unforeseen problem occurs. If the weather is rotten on Valentine's week this shouldn't mean there is no hope of meeting the year's sales target. Things do go wrong – you will make various screw-ups over the course of a year and there will always be some unexpected and unbudgeted costs. You must factor in some leeway – plan for some bad times.

After several years of travelling out to Silicon Valley to present good financial results the main board decided it would be a good idea if I moved out there to turn around an ailing part of our U.S. business. The package on offer was very tempting, with a much larger salary, two company cars (one for me and one for Liz) and all sorts of other benefits and bonuses. Liz came out with me for a week so she could look at houses and schools in the San Jose area.

This was twenty years ago now and the problem was that they wanted me to take an ailing part of the business, turning over not much more than $20 million, and grow it to $60 million in three years. I knew that it was absolutely impossible and, quite honestly, I felt that a lot of my success in Europe was largely down to good luck. I had benefitted from having a lot of great people working for me and a healthy customer base. The situation in the U.S. was much harder and the competition tougher.

I did entertain the idea of accepting the job, taking the money on offer and simply accepting that I was certain to fail. The company would probably fire me after three years but I would leave with a large pay-off. However, I knew I would face the prospect of three years of missing targets and all the flak and misery that went with this.

I had frequently sat in the boardroom and watched other senior managers taken apart in utterly merciless fashion for failing to 'make the numbers' and I had no desire to ever be on the receiving end of this sort of pain. It is the modern-day equivalent of being thrown to the lions and I saw the impact it had on people's lives and on their health.

As the owner of your own floristry business, you don't have to suffer the angst of trying to explain poor results to senior management. However you must explain them to yourself and maybe to your bank manager. So be honest and realistic and develop plans as if your livelihood depends on it – because it probably does.

I have met owners of florist shops who have no budget, no sales target and no profit target. They take the view that customers will either buy or they won't and there is little they can do to affect this. There are costs they know they will incur and they will try to be prudent in what they spend and hope they make enough sales to do okay. Well – this is no way to run any business and I've never met anyone who operates in this way whom I would consider to be successful. As the saying goes 'if you fail to plan, you plan to fail'.

Some of the best-known designer florists in the UK readily admit their business was a financial disaster in their early days. It was only after years of miserable financial results that they realised they had to get a grip on all the business fundamentals to eventually achieve real success.

If you do not have sales targets you have nothing to aim for. If you do not have a budget you have nothing to measure your expenditure against.

I cannot stress enough that I admire anyone with the talent to be a top-notch florist. I genuinely believe that just about anyone can learn the sort of stuff that I specialise in, but few have the innate talent to design and make beautiful floral products. If you are one of those talented types then please don't think you will never get your head around the business side of things.

Sales targets can be estimated by taking the shops previous year's actual sales, comparing this with previous years, and figuring out what the current trend is. You should try to quantify what you plan to do in the next year that will boost sales further. Think about how sales might be affected by your competitors, local circumstances and the economic forecasts for the country's economy as a whole. You should be ambitious but above all be wholly realistic.

Setting unrealistically high sales targets can be very demoralising when you consistently fail to meet them. Achieving them, or exceeding them, will give you a real buzz and the energy and enthusiasm to kick on.

If you need to raise finance from the bank you may draw up targets and budgets aimed mostly at impressing your bank manager. He will dissect the numbers and if he deems that your optimism outweighs your realism he will probably decide you are a bad risk. You have to produce numbers that you can justify and demonstrate that there is sufficient contingency for when things go wrong.

The budget for buying stock and paying for all the other operating expenses can also be calculated by examining previous years and then factoring in all the expected increases. Some of these will be known and some you will simply have to calculate based on the expected rate of inflation. Some will be affected by your own plans for making changes to your business. I always then added another small percentage to allow for the unforeseen extra costs that always occur in reality.

I love to watch those TV programmes featuring people starting a new business or developing an old property. It is usually fascinating to see their lack of realistic planning and their incredible optimism that everything will go according to plan. You then witness their angst when everything inevitably goes horribly wrong with huge cost overruns and missed deadlines.

If you have no historical data, because you are starting up a new business, then this is obviously more difficult and it involves a lot more guesswork. You will have to identify all the expected costs and calculate a budget that includes a good measure of contingency. New businesses usually greatly underestimate the costs involved, so try to find someone with real experience of starting a similar business who you can run things past. If you only talk to an accountant you will not learn enough about the nitty gritty that someone within the trade will know.

The profit and loss statement

There are a whole range of low cost, easy to learn and easy to use software packages available to make your accounting relatively straightforward these days. You can set up the details of your suppliers, account customers and the different types of sales and expenses. Once you get used to the system it is easy to spend a few minutes at the end of each day entering the relevant transactions for that day. Alternatively a couple of hours at the end of the week is all it takes to enter everything for the whole week.

With a few clicks of the mouse you can look at all your sales, stock purchases and operating expenses. This can be displayed graphically to show weekly, monthly, quarterly and annual totals and trends. It honestly is so easy – all the difficult stuff is done by the software. You can find out exactly what you have spent with each supplier and what each account customer has spent. Completing the quarterly VAT return takes a couple of minutes.

As mentioned in previous chapters, regardless of what your financial year is, it is possible to get an approximate P&L statement for the last calendar year with a couple of clicks of the mouse. The only time many florists get to see a P&L statement is when their accountant draws it up at financial year-end, and this is often several months after the actual year-end. This is a stone-age way of working in today's fast-moving business world.

All sorts of aspects of your business can change drastically in the space of a few months. By the time you realise that trends have changed and that there are problems that need addressing urgently you could already have wasted a lot of time and money.

A typical P&L statement for a healthy florist shop might look similar to the example on the following pages. This shows both the budget and the actual financial results for one financial year.

If you divide the gross profit by the total sales this gives you the gross profit margin, which is a healthy 49.25 per cent, given that it includes all the relay costs and sales. If you separate out all the relay sales and purchases then the gross profit is an extremely healthy 65 per cent.

If you divide the net profit by the total sales this gives you a net margin of 9.67 per cent which is very healthy given that the husband and wife owners are both paying themselves a wage from the business which is consistent with market rates.

180

All the figures in the P&L statement are net of VAT. Remember that VAT NEVER belongs to you – all you are doing is collecting money that is due to HMRC. People who claim they have received a totally unexpected and unfair demand from HMRC are often just being either naïve or dishonest. Of course, HMRC make mistakes like anyone else, but in my experience they are fair and reasonable to people who are playing the game and paying their dues.

Profit and loss statement for Apex Florist   **2016/17**

		Budget	Actual
Sales			
cash		59783	61284
cheques		13673	12946
credit/debit cards		252185	264731
relay		81823	79836
on account		54517	63288
	TOTAL	461981	482085
Cost of sales			
opening stock		7824	7221
purchases(relay)		98922	99378
purchases (stock)		138960	145719
less closing stock		-7289	-7415
	TOTAL	238417	244903
GROSS PROFIT		223564	237182
Other income			
bank interest		275	298
Overheads			
advertising		7500	6914
bank charges		536	549

card charges		2946	3177
cleaning & misc.		1312	1347
sundries		92	116
travel & subsistence		585	614
I.T.		3473	3619
insurance		1100	1113
staff welfare		680	717
light & heat		2789	2913
motor expenses		11694	12006
print,post, statnry.		946	972
rent		28000	27782
subs,books,training		480	447
telephone		5750	5913
prof. fees		160	216
wages		99681	102715
repairs&renewals		2458	2366
rates & water		13847	14016
	TOTAL	184029	187512

Depreciation

I.T. & f&f		1482	1378
motor vehicles		1946	1946
	TOTAL	3428	3324
Total operating costs		187457	190836
NET PROFIT		36382	46644

Sales Ledger

Modern accounting software will easily maintain a comprehensive sales ledger system which is the modern equivalent of the old double entry bookkeeping method. It enables you to see every order placed by an account customer, the payments they have made and their current balance. At the click of a mouse it can show the average number of days each customer takes to pay an invoice.

You can easily create professional invoices and statements. Again, at the click of a mouse you can look at every unpaid invoice that is more than thirty days overdue. You can examine how much each customer has spent over the past year and compare this to previous years.

This is a crucial aspect of any business as it is so important to the cash flow. It is no good clocking up lots of sales on account if you are not promptly invoicing customers and ensuring they pay as swiftly as possible. Many businesses are very slow to pay their bills and often the biggest companies are the slowest payers. They perceive this to be good business practice because it is beneficial to their cash flow.

It is no good having a seemingly healthy business which is racking up lots of sales if you are not getting the money in. As a small business, you will probably have to pay most of your bills very promptly so make sure you have got the cash to do this.

Many large businesses with healthy cash surpluses will not pay supplier invoices for three months or more, regardless of the stated terms of payment on the invoice. So even though you may clearly state that your terms are thirty days net many businesses will take absolutely no notice of this. After polite reminders, you may decide to try getting tough and charging them interest but the chances are they will simply ignore this or even drop you as a supplier.

Some customers will just sit on any invoice that does not meet their exact requirements as they see this as a justification for not paying it. Invoices need to specify accurately the details of each order. This should include the exact name and address of the business or person placing the order, the name of the recipient of the flowers, a description of the item ordered, the delivery date, amount and where appropriate a purchase order number.

Some large businesses will want separate invoices for each different department of their organisation that may have ordered flowers. Some want a separate invoice for each and every order and if you don't comply with their requirements they will delay payment until you do.

In our Cambridge shop I found that private individuals, the University colleges and most small businesses paid their bills very promptly. We had several large businesses who were consistently slow payers but who always paid in the end. I gave up trying to make them pay more quickly. Any problems we experienced with getting any invoice paid almost always related to an administrative problem, rather than any deliberate attempt to avoid payment.

Purchase ledger

This is very similar to the sales ledger but contains information about your suppliers. It records the details of every invoice they have sent you, the payments you have made and outstanding balances. It is an easy way to see how much you spend with each individual supplier and to compare how much you are spending on stock each week, quarter and year.

You can compare the ratio of stock purchases to sales, which is of crucial importance to your profitability. We would study these ratios every month and review what we thought of the deal we were getting from each wholesaler and whether we needed to take any action.

One month we suspected that one of our largest suppliers, whom we had been using for years, was starting to do some opportunistic overcharging. We rang round the other florists who we knew used the same supplier and compared notes with them. We established that they were indeed overcharging us and our complaints were immediately emailed to them. We detailed all our grievances and threatened them with the permanent loss of all our business. Their immediate response was a sizeable one-off credit against our next invoice, lower prices and a price list emailed to us the day before each future visit.

It is disappointing when something like this happens and it leads to a loss of trust in that supplier. We had been one of their largest customers and we always paid their invoices promptly so to be taken for a mug once was something we never forgot.

It is a source of frustration for many businesses that often a new wholesaler operating in their area will start by offering excellent services, prices and quality but that over time their performance gradually slides. You have to study the signals within your purchase ledger system to be able to quickly identify when this starts to happen.

Payroll

Ever since April, 2013 it has been compulsory for all businesses to report their payroll information in real time through HMRC's Real Time Information System (RTI). It is possible to calculate staff wages and make appropriate payments to HMRC, simply by using the free software available from HMRC. Just google

'Download HMRC's Basic PAYE tools' and it will work on pretty well any modern hardware/software platform.

You must be registered with HMRC as an employer and have a login for PAYE Online before you can start using Basic PAYE tools.

One thing it won't do is print actual payslips but if you are using accounting software such as Sage or QuickBooks then this can handle that for you very easily.

Every business must have an employer's PAYE reference in order to hire staff as without it you can't legally pay people or deduct PAYE tax and National Insurance Contributions. You can get this by calling 0300 200 3200 and completing the form over the phone. You will have to provide the basic details about your business, the dates on which you plan to start your first employees, when you will first pay them and how often you will pay them.

Use the online banking system BACS to transfer employees net pay directly from the business bank account to the employee's bank accounts. Your accounting software will automatically transfer all the payroll data straight into your accounts and make it easy for you to keep tabs on your staff costs as a percentage of sales. If you see that your staff costs are growing faster than your sales, then obviously this is something you must urgently address. Always compare your current staffing costs to your budget on a very regular basis.

I strongly recommend paying staff monthly as this is then a task you will only have to complete 12 times a year. Many employees would love to be paid weekly but why should you have to complete the task 52 times a year? Monthly payroll means less work and less paper. I found that once I was used to using Sage it took me approximately one hour to do absolutely everything necessary to pay eight employees and comply with all the requirements of HMRC.

You could simply get an accountant to do all this for you, but it is easy to do it yourself and an awful lot less expensive! When I sold one shop I had the whole payroll system set up in Sage – it was very easy to use and I offered to teach the new owner how to do it and to do the next couple of payroll runs with her. To my amazement she declined the offer and decided to use an accountant to do it all. I guess she decided she wanted to use her time only on the artistic floristry work.

Any employee aged over 25 must be paid at least the National Living Wage, which as from April, 2017 is £7.50 per hour. Employees under 25 must be paid at least the National Minimum Wage, which is again age related and the current bandwidths are as follows:

- Age 21 – 24   £7.05 per hour
- Age 18 – 20   £5.60 per hour
- Under 18   £4.05 per hour
- Apprentice   £3.50 per hour

One key decision you have to make is whether or not to pay staff when they are off sick. Employees who are off for more than four consecutive days are entitled to receive Statutory Sick Pay. They must notify you as soon as possible and supply you with evidence of sickness. You can recover the SSP against the amount paid for NICs.

You should be cautious of voluntarily paying staff for short periods of sickness. When taking over one shop I found there were a couple of florists who were in the habit of being sick on a cold wet Monday morning whilst their colleagues somehow always managed to get in. I quickly scrapped the voluntary sick pay and replaced it with a bonus scheme related to sales. Amazingly the health of these florists improved immediately and all the staff who were hardly ever off sick were pleased to earn more through the bonus scheme.

A pregnant employee can take up to 52 weeks maternity leave. The first 26 weeks are classed as Ordinary Maternity Leave and the final 26 weeks as Additional Maternity Leave. Leave can be taken up to 11 weeks before the expected date and must be taken for at least 2 weeks after childbirth.

Statutory Maternity Pay can be paid for up to 39 weeks. For the first 6 weeks this is payable (based on 2017/2018 tax year) at 90 per cent of their average weekly wage before tax. The remaining 33 weeks are paid at £140.98 or 90 per cent of their average weekly wage, whichever is the lower. Tax and NICs must be deducted and you have to pay SMP, even if you cease trading!

All these statutory payments are offset against the NICs that the business has to pay over each month. So if you were due to pay £500 in NICs for the month but you had paid out £120 in SMP you would make a net payment of £380.

Although as an employer you don't lose out financially when staff are pregnant, the biggest problem is often covering for their absence and planning your staffing for the future. You have to give the employee the right to return to work when they wish. Naturally many new mothers don't know if or when they will want to return to work.

I always joked with my staff that the business could only afford to have one employee pregnant in any financial year and I was very lucky that they complied with this!

Couples may be eligible for Shared Parental Leave and Statutory Shared Parental Pay and the details are easily found on the HMRC website. Dads can claim Statutory Paternity Pay and again all the details are on the website.

National Insurance Contributions will be calculated by your payroll software. Most employees will be classed as Category A which means that nothing is payable for the first £157 per week (at 2017/2018 rates). Above this level the employee must pay 12 per cent and the employer 13.8 per cent. For this reason many florists like to employ some people on a part time basis and keep their earnings below £157 per week. This often suits both the employer and the employee.

PAYE tax is also calculated by your payroll software. So long as you have entered the correct tax code for each employee this is straightforward. The software will utilise the current tax tables supplied by HMRC. Note that anyone with a BR (Basic Rate) tax code will not receive any tax free allowance and will have to pay the basic rate (currently 20 per cent) on all their earnings.

The year-end payroll procedure has been made much simpler since the introduction of RTI. Your payroll software will prompt you to enter the details of your final Full Payment Submission. This will usually be the March payroll or the last week's payroll for the tax year. You confirm it is your final submission of the year and answer the additional questions required for the final submission.

Your payroll software no longer needs to produce a P35 or P14 but it will produce a P60 for each employee which is a summary of payroll information, including your total earnings and the tax and NICs deductions for the year.

One relatively new aspect of payroll is Auto Enrolment. Most workers in the UK are going to be automatically enrolled into a workplace pension scheme by their employer. From the date they are automatically enrolled they have a month to decide whether to join or to opt out. If they do nothing they will be enrolled into the scheme. They will make contributions to a pension pot from their pay for as long as they are employed, or until they take their money out. Both employees and employers can contribute to build a retirement pot that is invested for the employee.

The minimum contributions are based on what is called 'qualifying earnings'. For the 2017/18 tax year this means that everything an employee earns in excess of £5,876 per annum is classed as 'qualifying earnings'. The amounts due from both employee and employer over the next three years are as follows:

Tax year	Employee	Employer
2017/18	0.8 per cent	1.0 per cent
2018/19	2.4 per cent	2.0 per cent
2019/20	4.0 per cent	3.0 per cent

Once again, your payroll software will handle all this for you.

Accounting ratios

You can keep a tight rein on your cost of stock and other expenses by regularly examining certain ratios. The most important one, which has already been referred to in previous chapters, is the gross profit in relation to total sales.

You also need to look at the total amount spent on stock, in relation to the total sales, for all the orders that were actually fulfilled by your business. By this I mean taking account of the incoming relay orders that you execute, but discounting the relay orders that you send out for execution by other shops. Thus you are examining the real cost of what you have to buy to fulfil all of your orders, including all the wastage. This ratio will vary from shop to shop but you should aim for circa 50 per cent.

If you are falling short then maybe you are paying too much for stock or wastage is too high or maybe your prices are too low.

Some florist shops are advertised for sale boasting some very impressive gross profit percentages but often this only reflects the way the owners have chosen to present their accounts. You have to examine exactly how they have accounted for all their sales and purchases. Only when you know just how they have accounted for their relay orders can you determine the real gross profit.

Once you know what the average is over a period of time, when the business is performing well and meeting your financial expectations, then you should aim to maintain this ratio at a similar level. Any creeping below the norm should worry you and make you examine the reasons why, so you can take some prompt action to get back on track.

It is also necessary to monitor the ratio of all the other operating expenses over which you have a level of control. You cannot usually do anything much about the rent once you have signed the lease, but the amount spent on wages and advertising is very much your decision. We found that the percentage we spent on wages grew steadily but there were good reasons for this. We wanted to fairly reward an excellent team of florists and as we got older we wanted to take more time off for golf and holidays.

From talking to other business owners and to business transfer agents, who have experience of selling many floristry businesses, we knew that we employed one more florist than was the norm for our level of sales. We were comfortable with this as it was our choice. We wanted to know for sure that we could get each day's orders made up and delivered well before 5pm, no matter how busy the day had been. Some florists operate with the absolute minimum number of staff which can improve profitability but leaves no margin for unforeseen problems. On a busy day, some shops are still delivering orders well into the evening and possibly turning away some late orders. I accept that for some people this is a necessary way to keep their heads above water financially.

We always knew that we might have to change and tighten the purse strings one day but while we were making a healthy profit we preferred to live with an above average wages bill. We were sometimes overstaffed on a quiet day but it meant we could cope on the very busiest of days.

Watching the advertising spend and keeping that to budget is also very important. Think long and hard about how many extra sales you would need to make in order to get a sensible return on the investment. In my experience, very few florists make a good return from any print advertising and I would advise putting your advertising pounds online.

Value Added Tax (VAT)

If your annual UK sales exceed £85,000 (this is the threshold for 2017/18) then you must register for VAT. You may find it advantageous to register even if sales are below this level as it gives your business more credibility.

If you are registered then you must charge for VAT (currently 20 per cent) on all your sales but you can reclaim all the VAT on your outgoings. I have previously stressed that a business should never regard the VAT it collects from its customers as its own money – you are simply collecting it for HMRC.

Your accounting software will strip out all the VAT from your accounts for the purpose of producing an accurate profit and loss statement. It will also ensure all the VAT is correctly accounted for and that the right amounts are paid to HMRC at the right time.

You have to complete a VAT return quarterly and you are allowed a month to submit this and pay whatever is due. HMRC has now phased out paper VAT returns and you must file it online and pay electronically.

Old fashioned businesses used to dread the VAT return. Proprietors would often spend a day (and often more) working through sheaves of paperwork, using a calculator, writing notes and doing a lot of cursing. Modern businesses let their accounting software do it with a couple of clicks of the mouse.

It really is incredibly easy if you have been entering your sales and invoices on a daily basis. Every quarter I thanked my lucky stars for my accounting software and chuckled when other florists told me they had spent all weekend on their return. People who don't use a modern solution seem to be amazed (and often horrified) when they finally complete all their sums and calculate what they owe. With modern accounting software, you will know your current VAT position on a daily basis and there are no unpleasant surprises.

To reclaim the VAT on all your purchases you need to ensure that you have a VAT invoice or a proper VAT receipt. This needs to specify the actual items purchased and not just the amount spent. An HMRC inspector will want evidence that all the items purchased really were items that you would realistically use within your business. A till receipt that does not specify the item purchased, even though it may have a VAT number on it, will not satisfy an inspector.

Capital allowances

Capital allowances are defined as money spent by a business on fixed assets and deducted from its profits before taxes are calculated. For the typical florist, this mainly relates to vehicles and fixtures and fittings.

For some businesses depreciation is one of the largest non-cash expenses. It is an important aspect of the accounts because it reflects the ageing of assets. Older assets will typically require more maintenance and repair as they age. As the depreciation of an asset increases the value of that asset will decrease. Most businesses will only account for this depreciation on an annual basis when they produce their P&L statement and balance sheet for the year.

Most small businesses use the straight-line depreciation method. This calculates an equal amount to be depreciated each year based on the expected life of the asset. For example, you may purchase a van for £15,000 (net of VAT) and assume that its useful lifespan will be four years and that you will then sell it for £3,000. You subtract £3,000 from £15,000 and the balance of £12,000 is your cost for the time you plan to own the vehicle. Divide the £12,000 by four to arrive at an annual rate of depreciation of £3,000.

Depreciation is obviously a real cost to the business. I have seen florist shops for sale where the owner claims that the depreciation should be classed as an 'add-back' from the P&L statement as it is just a theoretical amount for something which is already paid for. This is WRONG! To accurately reflect the decreasing value of assets is crucial to properly evaluate a business. You need to be constantly setting money aside for the day when that van needs replacing.

Many vehicles are now acquired on Business Contract Hire (BCH) with a down payment and then monthly payments over the term of a lease. This spreads the cost and as the vehicle is returned at the end of the lease it is never actually owned by the business.

Furniture and fittings are similarly depreciated on what should be a realistic assessment of their useful lifespan.

Tax inspections and record keeping

I have had a visit from an HMRC inspector to ensure that I was correctly processing everything with regard to VAT, wages, PAYE and NICs. This proved to be no problem as I was able to satisfy the inspector that I was using a reputable accounting system and that I knew how to use it.

The inspector randomly requested certain information and paperwork and I was able to find everything she asked for. If your files are in a mess, and it takes ages to find a particular invoice, they will not be impressed. Then you are likely to have a more prolonged and more detailed visit.

There were actually two ladies from HMRC who did the inspection and it lasted almost all day. I did my best to be friendly and efficient and keep them well supplied with tea and biscuits but it was obvious they were still going to do a very thorough inspection.

They particularly concentrated on everything related to the relay transactions as they had found out from previous experience that this was where many florists got things wrong. This didn't surprise me as I remembered that in the early days of owning our first shop I had found the Teleflorist financials fiendishly difficult to get my head around.

Our second shop used Interflora and I found their finance handbook was excellent. It was also a subject that was very well covered on their new members course.

Following our inspection HMRC wrote a report stating that there was just one area where they believed I had made a mistake and they said that I owed just over £100. I contested this as I genuinely believed they were wrong and they finally accepted that we did not have to pay anything.

Some years later I received another call from HMRC and on this occasion, they spent some time asking questions over the phone. It was evident that if I couldn't provide satisfactory answers then we would be receiving a personal visit. Thankfully they were pleasant and constructive and all was well. The thirty minute phone call was a big improvement on a full day's inspection. I don't believe they have the manpower to devote much time to each and every small business these days.

HMRC require you to keep business records for six financial years before you can destroy them. I find it is a real pain storing archive boxes in my loft but I know I can't afford not to keep it all. If the inspectors ever asked for it and I couldn't produce it I am sure they would make me pay dearly.

Doing the books – checklist

- Computerise EVERYTHING!
- Compare DIY benefits with using an accountant
- Create realistic budgets and targets
- Build in contingency for problems
- Constantly measure actual performance against targets
- Learn from your profit and loss statement
- Manage your sales ledger properly
- Use the purchase ledger to monitor supplier performance
- Opt for monthly payroll
- Study your accounting ratios and use them to adapt
- ALWAYS get VAT invoices and receipts for absolutely EVERYTHING and keep them
- Calculate depreciation properly and show it in the profit and loss statement
- Keep all records for at least six years

11 Relay Services

This chapter addresses:

- Traditional relay services
- Florist to florist
- A financial comparison of relay
- Alternatives to relay services

Whenever a customer wants to order flowers to be delivered outside of a florist's local delivery area this is typically relayed via one of the relay services such as Interflora.

This means the amount spent by the customer has to be split three ways: between the sending florist, the receiving florist and the relay service who are acting as the middleman. When all the sums are done the executing florist often receives as little as 60 per cent of the amount paid by the customer. Consequently the problem is how does the receiving florist, who has to do nearly all the work, make a reasonable profit on each and every incoming order.

In the modern era, it is possible for the customer to easily bypass both the sending florist and the relay services. A quick search on Google enables anyone to find a florist shop in the vicinity of where they want flowers delivered. BUT – many customers are duped by the results returned from their search engine and end up using a quite different service to what they are expecting.

The customer might think they've found an appropriate florist shop in the right place but may well be unwittingly using a centralised boxed delivery service. Many businesses are using the internet to give the customer a very false impression.

We will look at the way the traditional relay services operate and the alternative methods that are now available and compare the profitability for everyone concerned. The aim is to give guidance on just how you should best handle this relay dilemma for your business.

Traditional relay services

Interflora was founded in 1908 and our Cambridge shop was one of the founder members back in the early 1920s. It has become one of the strongest brands in the world and is a generic term for many people. Interflora claim that a staggering 82 per cent of consumers are aware of them. Many customers who contact a florist and ask 'can I send flowers through Interflora?' are really asking whether that florist can facilitate the sending of flowers to a remote location.

We have to remember that the need for, and consequent success of, the 'florist relay network' was born long before the age of the internet. The basic model was to create a national and international network of like-minded florists who all needed to send orders outside of their local area. In return, they would receive orders to execute locally.

The system worked as long as every florist was prepared to invest in getting their customers to place orders. They could offset the commission they earned against the commission they would give up on orders they received for execution. As long as a florist contributed to the system with outgoing orders the financials largely took care of themselves.

The customer paid an upfront service and transmission charge which went to fund the costs of running the network, building the brand and policing the quality and standards that were expected from all.

This model worked very well in the days before we even had the luxury of a fax machine. The Interflora communication network went on to be revolutionary in its time, allowing direct connection across the entire network of Interflora florists.

Our first shop used the Teleflorist relay service. When customers asked 'can you send flowers by Interflora?' we replied 'no, but we use a similar service called Teleflorist' and the customer was always willing to go ahead and place their order. They didn't care how we did it as long as we could get the flowers to where they wanted them to go. I never ever experienced one single customer who said they would prefer to find an Interflora shop.

Interflora are very protective of their brand name and take a very dim view of anyone who uses it incorrectly in their advertising or on their website.

There have been various different relay services over the years and many of these have either changed their name, been incorporated into another relay organisation or simply gone out of business.

When we took over an Interflora shop in the year 2000 we were one of over 2,000 Interflora shops in the UK who between them effectively owned Interflora. It was a non-profit making organisation in as much as the members were nominally in control. They empowered the board of directors to run the organisation in the most effective way.

In 2005 everything changed. The Interflora British unit changed from being a trade association to private equity ownership through the investment company 3i. Each of the member/owner shops received a pay-off but soon found that life was to be very different in the future. Many members had voted against the change and maintain a 'told you so' attitude to this day.

The new organisation would be very focussed on profit and the shops would have little or no say in how the new Interflora operated and in how they would be treated. In theory, the customer gets a good deal, with all the charges and commissions effectively being absorbed by the executing florist. However, when a third party is taking a large part of their profit florists are quite naturally tempted to cut corners on either the quality or the quantity.

The sending commission for a member taking and relaying on an order is actually very lucrative as there is little work involved. It is the poor old executing florist who has to bear the pain! It is little wonder so many florists much prefer outgoing orders to incoming orders.

Sadly for the florist, the relay operators of today tend to target all customers directly and endeavour to entice them to place future orders centrally. Florists have been concerned for years about giving away their customer's details when placing an order as this is tantamount to giving away your customer base.

This is why many florists feel that the original model of relay just doesn't work any more. Very few florists have high sending volumes these days. However, it is the poor old executing florist who has to really bear the pain.

When we were members of Teleflorist our incoming order volumes were very small. I found them relaxed about quite how we operated and what our quality standards were. So long as we fulfilled all our orders and paid our membership fees they seemed to have little contact with us. The Teleflorist organisation has since evolved into Eflorist.

When we sold this business and acquired a much larger shop, which was an Interflora member, it was quite a shock. The costs of membership were much higher and we had to pass a strict inspection before we were even allowed full membership. You must pay to attend the 'New members' course and Interflora will, for a period of time, retain some of the money you earn as insurance against you going out of business or terminating your membership.

All the conditions were much stricter and we regularly received test orders which were closely scrutinised and evaluated. The upside was that our incoming relay orders increased tenfold. We could not believe the huge volume of orders we received on our first Valentine's Day and Mother's Day as an Interflora member.

As time went by I studied the financials of Interflora membership more and more closely. I realised the net profit on each incoming order was tiny and we made a much better profit on our outgoing orders. We will examine the detail of the financials later in this chapter.

Since Incorporation Interflora membership has changed greatly. The individual members now have very little influence on how the organisation is run. I am told that many of them are unhappy about the flower count they have to comply with and the accessories they have to buy.

Some members say they now have to buy accessories they don't particularly like and which they then get stuck with when a particular collection comes to an end. During the last Mother's Day period shops sold out of one particular Interflora basket and were unable to order more. When individual florists attempted to buy something similar from another supplier, Interflora wanted them to send them a picture of the basket before they would approve its use as a substitution. This wasn't what members wanted to hear in the midst of a frantically busy peak period.

Every shop owner I have spoken to claims they are unhappy with the cut they receive and think that Interflora takes too big a slice of the pie.

On the plus side, members do benefit from a wide range of centralised support services, which use the muscle of a large corporation to obtain good deals for their member shops on various different essential services. Some members complain that they find themselves locked into contracts, even after resigning from Interflora, so read the small print before signing up to things like website hosting.

Interflora used to hold regular regional meetings and an annual conference for all members. We found that by really getting involved in these get togethers we learnt a huge amount from other shop owners. Sadly this seems to have gone by the board under the new organisation.

Some relay members now feel that their relay service provider actively discourages any kind of 'grouping' for reasons that can only be guessed at! There are however several closed social media groups which allow you to feel part of a community on both a business and a floristry level.

It used to be so interesting to talk to other members and compare notes on what works and what doesn't, and also what you wanted to try to get the central Interflora organisation to change.

Some Interflora members realise that although they make little or no profit on incoming orders it does enable them to turn over their stock faster. Consequently local customers benefit from a wider range of fresher flowers than would otherwise be possible.

Interflora claim that although incoming orders may not be very profitable they do contribute to all the other costs of running a florist shop. There is an element of truth in this but it also imposes certain costs on the business that would otherwise not exist.

It is no surprise that so many members don't particularly want incoming Interflora orders any more and an increasing number of orders are being fulfilled by Interflora centrally. These are made by less skilled staff in a warehouse and shipped out to the customer in a box. Although this alternative presumably makes very good financial sense to Interflora, it is very different to the traditional customer's expectation of a beautiful product, with visual impact, hand delivered by a local florist.

The number of Interflora members in the U.K. has now dwindled to around 1,500 but the brand name is undoubtedly still incredibly powerful around the world. In our Cambridge

203

shop we received many customer requests for flowers to be sent all over the world, and I must say I was always impressed by the organisation's ability to get flowers to just about anywhere and everywhere.

I can only imagine this must be a very worrying time for the relay services. In all my research for this book I have been unable to find a single florist who has come out of Relay and has subsequently regretted it. One very successful florist told me it was the single best business decision she had ever made!

Florist to florist

Over twenty years ago florists were regularly moaning about the traditional relay services and the poor deal they felt they were receiving. Whilst grateful that the relay operators provided the infrastructure for sending flowers around the world it seemed that most florists wondered why they couldn't use a simpler system. Shop owners talked to each other about how much better life could be if they could simply send an order to another shop without the need for a middleman who was taking a big cut of the proceeds.

This led to the birth of Florist2florist back in the 1990s, which then evolved into Direct2florist in 2007. A family owned business founded by florists who ran a number of shops in the north west of England. They set up a network of independent florists who wanted a better deal for both their customers and themselves.

Members currently pay an annual membership fee of £200 but they don't pay any commission fee on the orders sent and received. They do pay a transmission fee which contributes to central costs but it is nothing like the cut taken by a traditional relay service.

All of the flower value of each order goes to the receiving florist. The customer can pick the shop of their choice to make and deliver the end product, based on customer reviews and the information contained in each florist's website. Members can sell what they want at the price they want.

The biggest problem is that order volumes are relatively low and although there are now some 3,500 members, spread across 14 countries, this is very sparse coverage compared to the likes of Interflora. Thus many potential orders don't materialise because there is no member shop close enough to deliver to the intended recipient.

A financial comparison of relay

At the time of writing this the financial split of each order in percentage terms is as follows:

	Interflora	Eflorist
Sending commission	24.1	25.0
Executing commission	67.5	70.0
Marketing levy	8.4	5.0

I found an excellent analysis on the internet of the true cost of executing an Interflora order. This analysis was carried out by Lesley Nash, owner of Jennifleurs in Colchester. I visited Lesley at her shop and it was a model of how to present beautiful floral products in the most efficient way. Lesley is one of that very fortunate breed of people who have both artistic talent and a superb brain for business.

Whilst her team of florists were doing really top-notch make-up work Lesley sat at her computer demonstrating a complete grasp of the optimum way to run a very busy shop. If the owner of every floristry business was a Lesley this would be a very different industry indeed.

She made the very interesting comment: "Many florists are so busy with relay orders they lose sight of the financials – they confuse being busy with being successful". This really hits the nail on the head – there are lots of florists who are convinced they must be doing well as they have lots of orders and lots of work to do. They are so busy they don't have the time to analyse the profitability of what they are doing. Sadly a lot of these people are making little or no money.

Lesley used an example of a Valentine order for a dozen red roses, which at the time carried a price to the customer of £44.99 plus £5.99 delivery. A breakdown of the cost of flowers and sundries was as follows:

12 red roses	£13.92
Foliage	£1.00
Gyp	£0.55
Cello	£0.50
Ribbon	£0.08
Bag	£0.37
Tissue	£0.24
Care pack	£0.32
TOTAL	£16.98

Lesley calculated that it took a florist earning £7.50 an hour twenty minutes to make this and a delivery driver earning £7.00 an hour took twenty minutes to drive 5 miles to deliver it.

Interflora retained 32.5 per cent of the product price and £2.49 from the delivery charge, which came to a total of £17.11. Thus the executing florist's total cut was £33.87, but after paying £5.64 VAT the net amount was £28.22.

206

From this sum of £28.22 the florist had to deduct the following costs:

Materials	£16.98
Florist's wages	£2.50
Driver's wages	£2.33
Delivery costs	£2.25
I/F subscription cost	£0.65
Fee per order	£1.00
TOTAL	£25.71

Thus when all the sums are done the actual net profit for the executing member is £2.51.

This is without deducting any contribution towards all the other costs of running the business such as heat and light, rent and rates, insurance, I.T., telephone, marketing, employer's NICs and PAYE etc. It could be argued that these are all costs you have to bear anyway for the rest of your business, however really you should share the burden equally across all types of orders, both local and relay.

If a management consultant was analysing this they would also take account of other business factors. They would question whether you would need a similar sized shop if you didn't have a relay service and whether you would need as many staff. The conclusion would undoubtedly be that if you took everything into account you would be losing money on every order you executed.

It is interesting to compare this cost breakdown to how things would look if this order had been directly received by the florist instead of via Interflora. Assume that it is the same product sold to the customer at the same total price of £50.98 including delivery.

After deducting VAT of £8.50 the florist is left with £42.48 and from this amount has to deduct the following:

Materials	£16.98
Florist's wages	£2.50
Driver's wages	£2.33
Delivery costs	£2.25
TOTAL	£24.06

Thus the profit if executed as a local order is £18.42, compared to £2.51 if it was executed as an Interflora order.

My own personal view on Interflora is that before they became Incorporated it was, on balance, worthwhile us being a member, with around a third of our business coming from relay orders. However, if I still owned a shop now I definitely would not want to be an Interflora member. I would find a way to send outgoing orders profitably and I would not want to execute any incoming relay orders.

If I had terminated our Interflora membership I could have saved on the costs of two florists and potentially reduced the square footage of both the shop and the workroom. Given the situation now (post Incorporation) this would undoubtedly have made my decision a no-brainer.

Alternatives to Relay

I find that just about every florist I talk to these days has either quit relay membership or is thinking about quitting. Some have moved to a florist to florist service but although they are spending much less on membership fees and commission payments they are still not happy. Typically this is because they have problems with insufficient nationwide coverage and often, almost no international coverage.

So what should you do when a customer says they would like to send flowers a long distance? Some florists are taking a very honest and creditable stance. They are explaining what a poor deal a relay order is and telling the customer to find their own solution via a search engine. They are even explaining how careful you have to be when you search for a florist anywhere and how to avoid being duped by a boxed delivery service pretending to be the local florist shop.

This is a commendable approach but it makes no money for the florist. I don't see why you shouldn't provide a similar service to a relay organisation and give the customer a better deal whilst making a little profit for yourself.

You may feel uncomfortable with this idea and feel it unethical but I will explain how it works as I know there are shops doing this. They may work to different percentages but the idea has gained ground in recent years.

I am not for one moment suggesting you become the sort of 'virtual florist shop' mentioned earlier in this book, whereby you take a £50 order and then pass it on to another florist as a £20 order. This is dishonest and extortionate but it can work if you take a much smaller cut.

With a typical relay order the executing florist will receive some 67 per cent of the amount paid by the customer, so what if you simply relayed the order yourself and gave the executing florist 75 per cent? The customer would get a fair deal, the executing florist would get a better deal and you would get a better deal. The only person who loses out is the middleman who you have rendered redundant.

Let's take an example. A customer orders a hand-tied bouquet for £50, including delivery and VAT, to be delivered to a recipient at the other end of the country. You Google florist shops in that area and choose a shop that has very good reviews. You phone or email the shop and place an order for a £37.50 hand-tied, including delivery and VAT.

The tricky aspect is the VAT situation. The sending florist must pay the VAT of £8.33, received from the customer, to HMRC. If you can get a VAT invoice or receipt from the executing shop you will be able to reclaim the £6.25 VAT element of the £37.50 order.

When the sums are done this will represent a £10.42 profit for a sending florist if they can get a VAT invoice but only a £4.17 profit, if they are complying with the VAT regulations and can't get a valid VAT receipt or invoice. The receiving florist should be happy to provide this but once some florists understand what the sender is doing they may be reluctant to accept the order, let alone provide a VAT receipt. Usually this is because they suspect the sender is making a huge mark-up. It can be very frustrating and time-consuming to have to explain the rationale to the receiving florist. The fact is both florists are getting a better deal than they would if they had used a traditional relay service.

If you don't find this to your taste another idea is to charge up-front for the service you are providing. I know one florist who charges £7.50 for their time and the administration involved in sending an order to another florist. They make it clear that this is an up-front charge for their service and is regardless of the order value.

Of course, the VAT element of this must be deducted, leaving a net amount of £6.25 and you must try to get a proper VAT receipt or invoice from the receiving florist. This florist will only offer this service on orders to the value of at least £35 and tries to talk the receiving florist into waiving the delivery charge to get the best possible deal for their customer.

I think this is a commendable initiative from a florist who is prepared to make very little on outgoing orders in order to build loyalty with their local customer base.

Another alternative idea some florists are using is to handle the order themselves by sending a boxed delivery via a courier service. If you do this then the customer should be made aware of exactly what you are doing. If you show the customer a picture of a beautiful bouquet and then two days later they are complaining that they didn't know the recipient would be receiving a box from a courier, your customer may lose all confidence in you.

You could explain the problems of relay and try to reassure the customer that it is a tried and tested courier service and that the majority of recipients are quite happy with what they receive. I'm afraid that all these images on the internet of horrendous boxed deliveries would put me off this approach.

You have to respect the branding rights of a relay service, so if you bypass them, you shouldn't be using any old branded accessories or care packs, or even making any reference to them. You should, however, take the responsibility for the delivered product, so that if the customer does complain you make the same sort of replacement or compensatory offer that they would expect from an established relay service.

If you trawl the internet there are many postings from florists and customers about relay services and unfortunately most of what I have seen is very negative. Set against this however, it has to be acknowledged that there are many positive reviews from happy recipients.

I'm sure the relay services would claim that by using their services, customers can be confident they are getting the quality levels and flower content that they insist on. Whether this is true is questionable as I have heard tales of florists deliberately using cheaper and older stock for relay orders as it was the only way they could make a realistic profit.

The relay services would also claim that the customer benefits from their image and the assurance that any queries or complaints would be efficiently handled by a known and trusted brand.

If it makes any difference to the recipient whether their flowers arrive with Interflora or Eflorist branding, as opposed to their local florist shop, is open to question. I think that often this is down to what the reputation of their local florist is like.

I don't know what the future holds for the traditional relay service other than an increasing move towards centrally made box-couriered products. I suspect that through clever marketing on the internet many more orders are being placed centrally, rather than with a local florist.

It must be a major concern that so many customers seem to have realised that their best option is to use a search engine and find their own florist. I had previously thought that for sheer convenience many customers would take the option of letting a centralised relay service sort everything out for them. However, one florist stated that they had not had a single request to relay an order from any customer under the age of 60 in the last two years!

Probably the best advice is not to worry overmuch about relay but concentrate on building your local business by offering the quality, service and product USPs (unique selling points) that a centralised relay operation cannot match. Don't allow them to use you to furnish their business with elements they can't achieve without you.

Find a system that works for you with regard to servicing your local, regular customers. Focus on giving them a great deal so they come back to you. Unfortunately the days of making good money from relay orders are gone.

Relay services – checklist

- Compare the relay services
- Examine florist to florist as an option
- Carefully examine all the costs
- Do you want incoming orders?
- How can you make the most on outgoing orders?
- Do you want to send boxed deliveries?
- Do you want to opt for a DIY solution?
- If you stop taking incoming orders can you reduce staffing levels and shop/workroom space?

12 Staffing and training

This chapter looks at:

- Recruitment
- The florist's skill-set
- Staffing for peak periods
- Creativity and speed
- How many staff do you need?
- Training and qualifications
- Keeping current
- Driver skills
- Hiring and firing
- Trust and cooperation
- Communicating with staff
- Measuring productivity
- Health and safety

The world of floristry asks a tremendous amount of the people it employs and yet the financial compensation can seem very meagre. It is one of those industries which so many people want to work in that wages will always be modest. I was always amazed by the wide range of skills we looked for each time we took on a new florist. Somehow or other we did find people with a very broad skill-set who worked extremely hard, showed us great loyalty and were a joy to work with.

It is unfortunately a fact of life that most work which many people really love to do will not pay high wages. Thus florists are usually motivated to do work they really enjoy, even though they could earn similar pay stacking shelves in a supermarket. We always tried to provide the best wages and conditions that we could, but to stay competitive in retail floristry there is a limit to how far you can go. The higher your wages bill, the smaller your profits and it also reduces the price you can ask if and when you want to sell the business.

Recruitment

Floristry staff can often be found without spending any money on advertising. If you let your visiting wholesalers know that you need an extra florist they will spread the word at all the other shops they visit. If there is a local college running floristry courses they can be a rich source of trainees. We had some success with simply putting a notice in the shop window. When all else failed a small classified advertisement in the local paper always attracted some applicants.

The general reputation of your business will have a big impact on whether you receive applications from experienced local florists. If you have a reputation as a good employer, paying fair rates of pay, recruitment will obviously be much easier. Some florists seem to be continually advertising for staff and this makes the pool of local florists very wary as to why staff turnover is so high. Again, the wholesaler's grapevine effectively spreads the word about which businesses have happy staff and which don't.

When interviewing florists, you should obviously check their previous experience and qualifications and take up references. Telephoning a previous employer will usually reveal far more than a written reference. Because of all the legislation in place today most employers are reluctant to be at all negative in a written reference. A telephone call may well reveal that the applicant had a poor attendance and punctuality record or was not popular with their colleagues.

It is also a good idea to set a timed test for making up one or two products. A lot of otherwise experienced florists are slow in their make-up work. Someone who works slowly will prove frustrating and expensive. The productivity of your other staff may also slacken off as they question why they are working so quickly in comparison with the newcomer.

The florist's skill-set

When I first sat down to compile a list of the skills we wanted from a florist I was amazed at how long and diverse the list was. Quite apart from wanting people who had both design skills and the technical make-up skills essential for a competent florist, we wanted so much more.

A florist needs to have excellent selling skills, both over the phone and face-to-face with customers. They need I.T. skills to use the online systems in place and be able to produce lists of requirements and price quotations. They must be physically fit enough to be on their feet nearly all day doing make-up work, conditioning stock and carrying full buckets and vases around.

The use of English must be good enough to take and send orders around the world without spelling mistakes. A basic knowledge of world geography is also very useful for handling relay orders. Customer service skills will be tested to the limit when handling difficult customers and the many diverse complaints you inevitably receive. Looking after distraught relatives when they come to place an order for funeral flowers requires exactly the right balance of sympathy and selling.

Staffing at peak periods

At peak-times incredible levels of stamina are required to work long hours at a fast pace. I have previously mentioned the pressures I saw people exposed to in the I.T. industry. This does not compare with the sort of pressures that staff are subject to in a busy floristry business in the week leading up to Valentine's Day. I know this will be hard to believe for anyone who has not personally experienced it.

On a typical Valentine's Day we would start very early after just a couple of hours sleep. We would then work flat out all day and well into the evening with no breaks. We even found it difficult to find time to go to the toilet or drink a mug of coffee. We used all the labour we could find - extra florists and drivers and also general dogsbodies who could free up the florists to concentrate solely on selling and make-up work.

This comes after a week of working much harder, faster and longer than is the norm as all the orders pour in. I have honestly never experienced anything quite like it in terms of hard work and pressure.

Staffing at peak periods can be much easier if you have a number of staff who are prepared to work every day, and also do overtime, even if they are usually part-timers. We employed people who worked anything from two to six days in a normal week but they all worked a full week at peak times. Trying to find extra experienced florists for just a few days can be very difficult.

We were always very grateful that we had a workforce who told their families they would have to fend for themselves at Valentine's and Mother's Day periods.

Another attribute most employers require of their staff is to be proactive, rather than reactive. These words may seem overused but they relate to two very different types of personality. Proactive people generally make things happen whilst reactive people tend to have things happen to them.

As an example, assume that two different florists are given an order for a bouquet of lilies required for formal presentation at a function that day. The problem is that all the available lilies are tight and unlikely to open for some time. The proactive florist will call the customer, explain this and make alternative suggestions, or call a nearby florist to ask if they have any open lilies available. The reactive florist goes ahead and uses the tight lilies, hoping they will magically open and there will not be a complaint.

You need staff who will think ahead about anything that could result in a complaint and take corrective action to avoid any potential problems. If the day starts relatively slowly, with few orders, assume it will not last. Get the orders made up early and assume that lots more will flood in all through the day. Taking it easy early in the day can really rebound on you. It is much better to crack on with the work and then ease off later if it does turn out to be quieter than expected.

Creativity and speed

There are many people who can take a selection of cut flowers and make them into a beautiful bouquet or arrangement. Retail floristry means having to do this at speed. Something that might take an hour in a flower arrangers club will often have to be made in a few minutes in a busy florist shop.

The labour cost involved in making whatever your customers order is a vitally important aspect of a business either making a profit or running at a loss. It is no good having the most talented designers in the world if they take too long on the make-up work. Experienced florists can put together gift wraps in a few minutes. Hand-tieds typically take up to 15 minutes and arrangements in oasis perhaps 15-20 minutes or less, depending on the size. Of course, huge pedestal arrangements can take considerably longer.

Obviously increased speed usually comes with experience. However, there are people with a good eye for design and a good knowledge of flowers who never do achieve the sort of productivity needed in a business.

How many staff do you need?

The number of staff you need will depend very much on the people themselves and the nature of work in a particular business. I have seen florists who can make an average of six orders an hour and others who struggle to achieve half that.

Often an order that is being made up can suddenly become urgent. Perhaps the customer has arrived early to collect it, is parked on a double yellow line and wants you to really hurry. Some florists can put a spurt on and complete it quickly while others can suddenly become all fingers and thumbs.

If you have a small business with annual sales of less than £100,000 then on an average day all the make-up work could be done by one experienced florist. The problem is you also need to serve customers, answer the phone and buy and condition stock. This will typically mean you need a second person to help out and make the deliveries. So it is possible in a business this small to manage with one full-time florist and one part-time assistant/driver.

With annual sales of between £150,000 to £250,000 you will probably need three to four staff, including a driver. A larger business with turnover exceeding £300,000 will typically need at least five staff.

As turnover increases the wage bill, as a percentage of sales, should decrease. Sales per employee is a key element of the profitability of a business. They may be as little as £50,000 or less per person in a small business to over £75,000 per person in a large shop. Very large businesses, with annual sales exceeding £500,000, can find they reach a stage where sales per employee start to fall off slightly as each member of staff feels under a little less pressure.

There are exceptions to these guidelines in well run businesses where the management control is very good and staff motivation high. In large florist shops in the U.S. it is common to see league tables on the work-room notice board showing the productivity of each individual florist. Staff compete to be top of the league and win awards and bonuses.

Training and qualifications

Most florists acquire their skills through a combination of formal training and hands-on experience. It has to be acknowledged that some of the UK's most talented florists are self-taught but they are very much in the minority. There are a whole wealth of excellently illustrated books available showing the techniques for making up all types of floral bouquets and arrangements. I have just searched Amazon and found 426 of them!

There are both classroom courses and online courses. They range from free college courses, all the way through to a four-week course at a private floristry school in London costing £5,200. For most people, the obvious route is to find a local college offering floristry courses, do practical work from home and try to find a position as a trainee or 'Saturday person' at a local floristry business.

At present, there are around a hundred UK colleges that offer floristry courses. Some of these are specialist horticultural colleges with purpose built facilities. Some are general colleges of further education and some use any available facility such as local community centres.
You can study full-time or part time, depending on just what is locally available. School leavers who want to acquire the full range of floristry background and skills can opt for a full-time course, as can mature students who might want a change of career. My local college offers courses ranging from one-day workshops through to a two year full time course.

Jenny started with a one-year foundation course at Otley College, which really gave her the flower arranging bug. She moved on to do the C&G 7900 Creative Studies Part One Flower Arranging Skills, followed by the Part Two Extended Flower Arranging Skills.

She was then offered her first floral teaching work with Adult Education, offering six-week leisure courses. This was followed by a further one year C&G 7802 Training and Development course which enabled her to gain the Training and Development (Level 3) in Further Education Teaching Certificate. This course was very popular at the time but when funding for mature students came to an end the numbers really dropped.

Jenny continued to teach leisure classes and day workshops whilst developing her Flowering Passions business, doing floristry for weddings, events, contracts, flower festivals and also sympathy work. She developed a real interest in competition work and worked together with Roger Woolnough to win a gold medal at Chelsea. She has also won 'Best in Show'

221

at the Suffolk Show. At the time of writing this she has just been working with her friend and ex-student Di Siddall on a large scale design, which has resulted in another first prize at the Suffolk Show.

Floristry is a wonderful industry for building personal relationships. Jenny developed ongoing friendships with many of her students, including a Japanese lady who was in the UK for a year to study floristry. She spoke very little English but they found the language of flowers united them. They did lots of one-to-one sessions on the written work which enabled this lady to eventually gain her qualifications. Jenny has remained friends with her ever since and she has been over from Japan to visit.

For those wanting to pursue a work based route rather than going to college there are government funded apprenticeship schemes. Typically this is aimed at people already working within the floristry trade who want to supplement their practical skills with a deeper understanding of all aspects of floristry.

Formal floristry qualifications are grouped into 5 different levels as follows:

- Level 1
  Certificate in Land based studies – floristry route (CF)

- Level 2
  National Certificate in Floristry (NCF)
  First Diploma in Floristry
  NVQ2 Floristry and Key Skills

- Level 3
  Advanced National Certificate in Floristry (ANCF)
  National diploma in Floristry
  NVQ3 Floristry and Key Skills – Technical Certificate

- Level 4
  Intermediate Certificate Society of Floristry (ICSF)

222

Higher Diploma in Floristry (HDF)
Foundation Degree (HND)
NVQ4 Floristry and Business Management

- Level 5
  National Diploma Society of Floristry (NDSF)
  Master Diploma in Professional Floristry – Degree

The academic qualifications needed to qualify for the very popular Level 2 Diploma in Floristry course is 4 GCSEs at grades D/F, including grade D/3 in English and Maths.

The Level 3 Extended Diploma in Floristry is very much aimed at those wanting a career in retail floristry. The entry requirements are 4 GCSEs at grade A to C, including English and Maths at grade C or above.

Further detail on floristry education and training can be found on the BFA (British Florist Association) website.

My first wife Liz achieved the Level 4 ICSF qualification and then wanted to move to Level 5 NDSF but she became so busy running her own shops that she had to put this on hold. She really rated the course she did at Hadlow College to achieve ICSF and always thought it had given her the necessary foundation to move on to running a successful floristry business.

Keeping current

No matter how talented you and your staff might be, you always have to keep up with the latest trends and developments within the industry.

I would say it is absolutely essential to have an online subscription to The Florist magazine. I have always found this a mine of information about what is going on and the editorial team don't pull their punches. If they think florists are not getting a good deal they will say so, even if that may infuriate the relay operators!

They have lots of articles about changing trends, new techniques and innovative products. They are not afraid to have a go at florists stuck in the past who seek to moan about their problems, rather than making changes to the way they do business. They have developed the Good Florist Guide which enables anyone to find a florist that has been checked out for quality and excellence.

The BFA (British Florist Association) offer similar information and services to all professional florists and have a florist-to-florist communication network. They took over the old Society of Floristry in 2010 and provide lots of information on training, qualifications and competitions. Membership is currently £80 per year.

Driver skills

When taking on delivery drivers previous experience is always preferable, because it is one thing to be an experienced driver and quite another to efficiently handle city centre deliveries. Satnavs have obviously made the task of finding addresses much easier but local knowledge can still improve upon the typical satnav chosen routes.

Delivery drivers know the best routes to take at different times of day and make allowances for school hours and known bottlenecks. They know that you cannot always park correctly and legally when dropping off an order. They are streetwise enough to know what they can get away with to avoid problems and keep to deadlines. To make deliveries in busy towns and cities without ever infringing any regulations would take forever.

A driver needs to be clean and smart and confident enough to make appropriate small talk with the recipient. They must be careful to avoid any damage to the product being delivered and can give basic advice about caring for flowers. Handing over flowers with a cheery 'Happy birthday' or 'Happy anniversary' always goes down well.

If the recipient isn't at home then the driver should either find a safe shaded place to leave the flowers, or leave them with a neighbour and put a card through the recipient's door, telling them where their flowers are. I always instructed our drivers that on no account were they to ever bring an order back with them – knocking on ten doors is always preferable to having to make another delivery run later in the day.

At peak-times I paid casual drivers by the delivery and if they brought anything back they didn't get paid for that order!

Hiring and firing

All members of staff must have a contract. This should state their rate of pay, the hours they are expected to work, holiday entitlement, details of sickness pay and the period of notice due for termination of employment. Both the proprietor and the employee need to sign this document and each should retain a copy.

In the event of unsatisfactory performance you must follow the correct disciplinary procedures to ensure you do not leave yourself open to a charge of unfair dismissal. The propensity of 'no win, no fee' services available has encouraged many people to seek financial compensation, often regardless of the real reasons relating to why they have lost their job.

If you make someone redundant you have to put them 'at risk' first. This means telling them their job is not secure and consulting fully with them before any notice of termination is given.

If an employee is upset by banter between their colleagues you have to take action to put a stop to this. There is always banter in a busy floristry business and much of it is of a sexual nature. I've never known anyone I worked with being upset by this, and I was often the only man working in a shop with up to eight women. I found it to be much the same as working with men and the jokes were just as blue. I was always pleased that the girls felt comfortable enough not to feel the need to change their usual behaviour.

When the girls went on holiday they would usually send a racy postcard back to the shop. So that I wouldn't feel left out they would also send me one, often showing a nude woman. All these went up on the workroom wall and nobody was ever offended. However, if you do have an employee who is upset by this sort of thing you must take corrective action. Any cases of sexual harassment are usually found in favour of the plaintiff.

Employees need to know that if they do have a grievance they can talk to their manager about it. The details of the grievance, and any agreed action, must be carefully documented.

An employee who is being disciplined, and is a member of a union, has the right to be accompanied by a union representative at any disciplinary hearing. Even if an employee is caught stealing, and they admit to it, instant dismissal is not possible. The disciplinary process must still take place.

If an employee wants to work flexible hours, perhaps because they have young children, and this doesn't fit in with your plans,

226

there is a strict procedure to follow. Parents have many rights these days and the law expects employers to be sympathetic to their needs.

As an employer, you should keep a separate personnel file for the routine information you hold on each employee. The Data Protection Act requires that highly sensitive data, such as doctor's certificates produced for absence, should be kept separately.

Trust and cooperation

We have covered some of the aspects relating to the regulations for unsatisfactory performance. I have always found that the usual relationship between employee and employer in a typical floristry business is much more likely to be one of trust and friendship.

It is very easy for anyone handling direct customer sales to pocket cash occasionally instead of ringing it up on the till. In a florist shop it can be very difficult to catch anyone doing this. If it is a transaction that has an order form related to it then there will be an audit trail. This enables you to check that it has been paid and accounted for. In fact, this is an essential task at the end of day to ensure that all the orders have indeed been paid for. It is very easy on a busy day to forget to put an order received over the phone through the card machine.

However, when a customer dashes into the shop for £10 worth of cut flowers and slaps a £10 note on the counter before dashing out again, this can be a tempting opportunity for anyone who is not totally honest.

We were very lucky in employing people we trusted completely. By treating your staff well and rewarding them fairly you are much more likely to build up two-way trust and friendship.

The only time we have ever doubted anyone we employed was some years ago when we found that the till was often £10 or £20 short at the end of the day. By studying which members of staff were working on days when the till was short we narrowed it down to two suspects. The problem was that the till was only ever short on days when both these members of staff were working. We suspected this was a deliberate ploy so that we would never be able to pinpoint just one individual. The problem was eventually solved when both these employees left of their own accord and from that day the till was never noticeably short again.

In our Cambridge shop we built up a team of florists whom we trusted 100 per cent. All of them were good customers as well as employees and would take advantage of the 20 per cent staff discount we gave them. They were all so scrupulously honest that when they paid for anything they would always get a colleague to ring it up.

The shop closed officially at 5pm each day but often we would have late customers and this often meant one of the staff could not leave until perhaps 5.30pm. I would always thank them for staying late and promise to add half an hour overtime to their pay but they would usually tell me not to bother. You are unlikely to get this sort of commitment unless you reciprocate by treating your staff well. It is essential to give them the respect and recognition they deserve.

Communicating with staff

At the end of each peak period Liz and I would always thank all the staff personally for all the exceptionally hard work they had put in. We would also put our thanks in writing when giving them an appropriate bonus.

Communication with your staff is vital in any sort of business. Quite apart from the day-to-day chat in the shop it is important to put things in writing on a regular basis. At the end of each month I gave each of our staff a memo summarising how the shop had performed in that month. Usually this was a 'well done' memo but if our average order value had dropped below par this was spelt out. There would be a reminder that we all had to keep working at this and ensuring that we were offering the full range of prices and add-ons etc.

The monthly statistics provided by Interflora were always of interest to all the staff. These showed our sales, order values, comparison with the previous year and our ranking in the league table. Every month I posted this on the workroom noticeboard.

At the end of each year we would give each employee a memo summarising how the shop had performed in that year. It also explained our aims and objectives for the coming year as I found that they were genuinely interested in the big picture. If the staff are properly involved they will offer all sorts of good ideas about how things could be improved.

Employees will feel more involved with the wider world of floristry if you make relevant magazines and product and supplier brochures available to them. We always made the current copies of all the floristry and flower magazines available to them.

Measuring productivity

I have mentioned previously in this book that floristry businesses in the U.S. have a much more competitive element to them when it comes to evaluating the effectiveness of staff. Having worked for American I.T. businesses for most of my working life I have always been interested in the cultural differences within the workplace. It is interesting to look at how things are typically done in a U.S. floristry business.

When Liz and I visited florist shops in the U.S. they were always happy to show us behind the scenes and talk about their working methods. Usually their staff were either 'salespeople' or 'designers'. They used the term 'designer' for anyone capable of doing make-up work. They were always surprised to hear that in the U.K it was more common for anyone working in a florist shop to be a 'jack-of-all-trades' – serving a customer one minute and making a bouquet the next.

American shops tend to focus very much on developing a competitive element to all their work. It is common to see a big whiteboard on the workroom wall showing league tables of the employees. They track how many products are made by each designer and the average time taken to make each different type of product. There are bonuses for achieving set objectives and some sort of prize for the league leader. It is common to see somebody proudly wearing the 'designer of the month' or 'salesperson of the month' badges.

The staff seem to accept this way of working because they know it is commonplace. I always got the impression that they thought we were incredibly laid-back in the U.K. when I told them this wasn't our usual practice. They would ask us 'how do you know who your best people are?'

For their 'salespeople' the league table would show the number of orders taken by each person and their average order value. Often there is a special monthly prize for the biggest single order taken. There is a lot of chat about this as individuals seek to win it with perhaps a big wedding or funeral order or often some large corporate event.

Whenever I suggested adopting a similar scheme in our shop the staff were always against it. Their view was that it would damage team morale if they were all seeking to outdo each other and that it would be humiliating for whoever came bottom of the league.

I offered to fund bonuses and prizes but I couldn't win them over and didn't want to impose it against their wishes. They were each doing a good job and morale was excellent so I didn't want to rock the boat. They made the point that such a scheme could be counter-productive with people not wanting to take what looked likely to be low value orders. They also thought there could be arguments over whose turn it was to answer the phone next.

Eventually we settled on a compromise scheme that tracked the total order volumes and average values. All the staff shared a bonus for beating the average from the corresponding month in the year before. This did work well in as much as the average order value did consistently improve.

To be absolutely honest I am still not sure to this day whether I did the right thing in the interest of team morale or if I took the wimps route by not daring to upset the apple cart!

Health and safety

I appreciate that this isn't everyone's favourite topic but most aspects of H&S are just common sense. It doesn't have to be costly, complicated or time consuming and the Health & Safety Executive supply all the detail you need. Much of it is free of charge and available online.

As an employer, you must provide a reasonable standard of health and safety for your staff and also for any visitors to your business. H&S inspectors have the right to enter your premises to carry out an assessment and enforce legal requirements.

When setting up a business you must:
- Inform your local authority of the business name and address
- Display the H&S law poster in a prominent place
- Display the employer's liability insurance certificate in a prominent position.
- Appoint (and provide training for) a First Aid officer.
- Produce a written statement on policy for H&S for your staff and then regularly review and update it.
- Ensure everyone in the workplace is aware of risks and understands the procedure to follow when accidents occur.
- Assess the fire risks of the workplace and keep a written record.

To provide a safe working environment you should check that the exits and entrances are always kept clear. Fire extinguishers should be examined annually and electrical fittings and equipment checked.

A fully stocked first aid kit must be made available to all staff, together with a book for recording all accidents and any action resulting from them. Chemicals must be clearly labelled and stored safely. Appropriate protective clothing must be provided.

Your local HSE office can provide you with free booklets on the H&S regulations and H&S law.

When our shop was inspected by staff from the local HSE office we actually found them extremely helpful. They gave me good warning of their visit and I spent half a day preparing for it. This mostly involved reading the booklets and producing the necessary paperwork. They made a thorough inspection of the premises, my paperwork, the H&S posters, the first aid kit and all the fire extinguishers. The only action I had to take was to fit a safety chain to secure the helium bottles (for inflating balloons) to the shop wall.

As an employer a lot of this can seem very picky but sometimes it really is in your interest to comply with it. If you have taken reasonable steps to prevent accidents, or harm coming to your employees, then you shouldn't be responsible for the payment of any compensation.

There are some particular hazards for the florist. Floral foam products can contain some quite toxic chemicals and for this reason boxes of it should not be stored above eye level. When a block of foam is pulled out of the box the dusty residue can cause irritation to the eyes.

Most plant materials are poisonous so always wash hands well after working with them and avoid touching the face and eyes. Plants like euphorbia exude a milky sap which can irritate the skin and be very painful if they come into contact with the eyes. Splash with cold water and seek medical help if necessary.

Hyacinth bulbs can also cause problems and should only be handled while wearing gloves. Plants with hairy stems are notorious for causing skin irritation.

House plants can also be harmful to pets – cats and dogs brush against them and then lick their fur, which can cause problems. Be especially careful with lily pollen.

Everyone knows that some flowers are poisonous and when a florist's hands come into contact with their mouth, after handling them, it is easy for serious problems to develop.

Wikipedia lists a total of 64 flowers which are known to be poisonous. One internet listing of the seven most deadly flowers includes some very common flowers, such as foxglove and lily of the valley. Anthuriums contain needle-like crystals which can penetrate the skin and cause discomfort. They contain proteolytic enzymes which release histamine and kinins, causing swelling and itching or a burning sensation. Any swelling is best treated initially with a cool compress.

There are lots of freely available posters on the internet, showing which flowers are poisonous, that can be printed off and displayed on the workroom wall.

Staffing and training – checklist

- Try the free methods for recruiting before spending money on advertising
- List the full skill-set you need for each position
- Plan staffing carefully for peak periods and err on the side of caution
- Recognise the value of staff productivity, particularly with regard to make-up times
- Keep your staff levels in line with the industry norms, based on turnover
- Understand the value and significance of the different floristry qualifications
- Utilise the full potential of a delivery driver to maximise the experience for the recipient
- Stick to the rules for hiring and firing
- Build true trust and cooperation with all your staff
- Keep all staff informed of just how the business is performing
- Set up measures for productivity and constantly monitor them
- Keep to the HSE rules and guidance to protect both yourself and your employees
- Know which flowers are poisonous, and may present a health risk, and communicate this to your staff

13 Deliveries and complaint handling

This chapter addresses:

- Scheduling deliveries
- The delivery process
- Unusual deliveries
- The cost and price of delivering
- Peak period delivery planning
- Handling complaints
- Relay order complaints
- Assessing complaints
- Delivery problems
- Complaints of short product life

Many people think that delivery is the easy routine part of the floristry business, the part that comes after all the difficult design and make-up work has been done. However, every floristry business owner knows this is a key part of the industry and that it requires a lot of thought to handle efficiently.

I often used to daydream about how simple life would be if all our customers came to the shop, bought something and took it away with them. In the floristry world these sort of customers are very much in the minority.

Deliveries can and should involve much more than the main tasks of loading up, finding the right addresses and handing over the product. I quite enjoyed making deliveries as it was an opportunity to brighten up the recipient's day and make someone happy. Also at very busy times it was nice to escape

235

the hustle and bustle of the shop. Of course, it can be anything but fun when you are racing against the clock and stuck in traffic.

Scheduling deliveries

At the end of each day we would write up the delivery schedule for all the orders we had for the following day. The delivery sheets were headed with the date and divided into columns with the following headings:

Sequence – This was for entering the numerical sequence for each delivery, based on the location and whether or not it was a priority delivery, that had to be delivered within a particular time window.

Recipient name

Address – Any address that was for a road or street name we did not recognise, or for a house with a name but no number, would be checked before leaving the shop. Finding a house by name in a long road can waste a lot of time. Postcodes should always be used as most satnavs will at least get you very close to the exact address.

Time required – Most deliveries will be made at any time during normal working hours. Customers may pay extra for morning or afternoon delivery or for a particular time window.

Time delivered – We always logged an exact time that did not look like an approximate time. For example, a delivery made at 1000 would be logged as 0959 or 1001. We found this helped to convince a customer that you really did know precisely when it was delivered.

Left at – This was for the many occasions when the recipient was not at home and the order had to be left in a secure place or with a neighbour.

One column we did not have was for acceptance of delivery. We didn't use this unless the customer had explicitly requested it. While some people are happy to sign, some regard it as an annoyance. The porters at the University colleges in Cambridge were often reluctant to sign for flowers. They would often sign as Micky Mouse or Donald Duck as they didn't want to take responsibility if anything went wrong. Busy hospital nurses would often regard it as a frustration they could do without.

Only once did we ever have a problem concerning signatures and yet the time saved by not asking for one was covered many times over. I know some florists will disagree with me over this and relay companies will usually insist on a signature.

Satnavs have been a real boon to the delivery process and there are plenty of products that will work out optimum delivery sequences for you. I used to use one called Route 66 but once I really knew the Cambridge area well I figured it out for myself, using local knowledge of the best routes to take at different times of day.

At the end of each month we filed all the delivery sheets and we actually kept them for at least a year as sometimes we would get a query about a delivery made many months ago. Many people who send flowers are absolutely convinced the recipient will phone to thank them immediately the delivery has been made. If this doesn't happen they assume the florist has failed to deliver it. Filing delivery sheets is a quick way to deal with this very frequent problem.

The delivery process

Loading deliveries into the van is a good opportunity to check a number of things. I used to double check that each order had all the correct attachments, such as a message card in an envelope, care card, gold card, flower food, bow etc. A code letter on the message envelope showed what attachments should be with the flowers, such as balloon, champagne, teddy etc.

I would also look at the order to satisfy myself that it looked right.

If a £30 bouquet didn't look like £30 worth I would ask the florist who made it to just double check the flower content. Almost always we would find it had been correctly made up but because of perhaps the choice of flowers, or unusually high current prices, it looked smaller than usual. Sometimes we would decide to add a couple more stems anyway to improve the appearance of value for money.

I believe these sorts of checks and comments are something any experienced delivery driver can and should make. Obviously they need to be made tactfully, and with respect, to the florist who made up the order.

The driver must be very careful to protect deliveries that have to be kept upright in the van. Some drivers cut holes into thick polystyrene to slot the orders in securely. I preferred to cut holes in the top of the large cardboard flower boxes we received from wholesalers. I would cut different sized holes for hand-tieds and vases. Each time Interflora changed their collection I would cut new holes to fit the new products.

I was subjected to a lot of mickey taking from the girls about my boxes, as they would enquire if I had patented my latest version. At one of the shop's Christmas dos they presented me with a certificate for 'Saddest Job of the Year' for my boxes. In my defence things rarely fell over when I was delivering.

When handing over flowers to the recipient I was always aware of the occasion and tried to adopt appropriate behaviour. If it was a birthday I would smile and wish the recipient 'Happy Birthday' and resort to shameless flattery if there was a balloon with their age on it. If it was sympathy flowers then I would simply be polite and respectful.

It is often a good idea to give some basic care advice when handing flowers over as often people don't read the care card. Some people think they can wait a day before getting flowers into water.

It is obviously essential for the driver to have a mobile phone as communication with the shop is often necessary. A quick call for a check on the computerised addressing system will often show that the sender has got the house number wrong. An order returned to the shop usually means an extra journey to the right address later in the day.

Sometimes the shop will call the driver to tell them not to deliver a particular order because another order has come in for a nearby address. This can save two long trips to an outlying village in the same day. Drivers become adept at adjusting and optimising the delivery sequence as circumstances change throughout the day.

Unusual deliveries

Deliveries can sometimes be quite funny. I once made a delivery to a couple who had just moved in to a new mobile home near Cambridge. They saw me arrive and a man came to the door to warn me there was wet cement below the door. As he reached over to take the bouquet his hand slipped from the door and he fell headlong into the wet cement. When I got back to the shop I checked the message on the order – it read 'Good luck in your new home'.

One customer proposed to his girlfriend by sending her red roses every day for two weeks. Each delivery was accompanied by a one-word message on a card. Only when she received the last delivery was the proposal message complete. Aren't us men just fantastically romantic?!

Another customer walked into the shop and asked how much our bouquets cost. When we replied that they mostly ranged in price from £20 through to £100 he said he would like one for £110. As well as having the bouquet delivered he also wanted me to deliver a diamond engagement ring with it. I was to phone him immediately after I had handed them over to tell him what the lady's reaction had been. Fortunately she was delighted, the answer was 'Yes' and some months later we did the flowers for their wedding.

Some deliveries are not so pleasant. I once delivered flowers from a distant son to his elderly mother and she broke down in tears. She told me she was suffering from depression and begged me to stay and chat to her as she hadn't spoken to anyone for days. I talked to her for as long as I could spare and then called her son to explain, hoping he would visit her soon.

On another occasion I delivered to a lady who was absolutely terrified because a robin had flown into her house and she had a phobia about birds. She shut me in her lounge until I could get it out of the window.

It pays to make it clear that you are delivering on behalf of a florist. This is easily done by wearing a jacket with the business name on and by parking your nice clean sign-written van right outside. People are usually very pleased to let the neighbours see that they are receiving a flower delivery. If you have to deliver something in your private car you don't want a lady's husband suspecting you are up to no good!

240

One of our nicest deliveries was a bouquet for a little girl on her seventh birthday. Apparently it had always been her ambition to have flowers delivered to her. She had seen her mum receive bouquets and thought it was really cool and grown up. I parked the van right outside the front door and announced that I had a delivery for Miss Jones – her face was a picture.

We received regular orders from customers overseas who wanted flowers placed on relative's graves. Many of these were from the US for relatives buried in the American War Cemetery just outside Cambridge. After placing the flowers on the grave, I would take a picture on my phone and email it to the sender. This confirmed that we had carried out their wishes and resulted in some really lovely thank-yous.

The cost and price of delivering

The advantage of handling your own deliveries using your own staff, and your own vehicles, is that you have full control. A clean van with striking signage can be a wonderful advertisement for your shop. However, at peak times you have to use other drivers as well. You may decide that delivering is a headache you would like to outsource to someone else.

In Cambridge, when we were typically charging between £4.50 and £6.50 per delivery, we were approached by a firm who offered to do unlimited deliveries at £2.50 per drop for anywhere within a ten-mile radius of the shop. This was a fantastic offer, which we took full advantage of at busy times. Even with our two vans I couldn't see how I could have handled these deliveries at such low cost.

At the time of writing this, the delivery charges levied on Interflora orders are as follows:

Standard charge - £6

AM or PM - £10

Same day within 3 hours - £13

Note that Interflora retain part of this delivery charge – as an example they keep £2.49 of the £6 standard charge. Thus the £3.51 which goes to the delivering florist is a very meagre amount and very unlikely to cover the real cost.

I would suggest that the amounts charged by a florist for local orders, that they have gathered themselves, need to be close to the full Interflora charges to enable a business to cover this cost.

Peak period planning

While one van will suffice for many businesses to handle all the deliveries on a typical day, everyone needs extra capacity at peak times.

You can take advantage of friends and relations who are prepared to help out. I found this really only cost effective if they had a suitable vehicle of their own and were appropriately insured. Hiring extra vans for a day or two is relatively expensive. The best solution for us was to book our low-cost delivery service and pay them by the drop.

In the run-up to a peak period we would double check all the address details. These were written on the message card envelope, together with the delivery date, which was attached to the order form. At the end of each day I would go through these and write an area code in the corner of the envelope. CC for Cambridge Central, CN for Cambridge North, E for a village to the east etc.

Once each order was made up the florist would check that all the attachments were there. The order would be placed in a designated area corresponding to its particular area code. Every available space was used, including the office and the storage sheds. Any timed deliveries would be prominently placed at the front of each batch of orders.

On peak period days I didn't do any delivering myself. I spent all my time organising all the extra drivers, allocating them to areas they were most familiar with. I helped them load the orders, made up the delivery sheets and ensured they knew about which orders had to be delivered by a certain time.

New orders would be coming in all the time and so the situation was very fluid. Lots of make-up work was in progress and new orders had to be placed in the right areas. I checked and double checked the orders continually to ensure that no order had been misfiled or obscured somewhere.

As well as taking responsibility for all the orders that your shop needs to make up and deliver, you also have to keep an eye on the status of all the relay orders you have sent. These should be taken care of and delivered by the executing florists but it is well worth doing all the checking you can. By using the Interflora online system we were able to check that each order we had sent was formally accepted and delivered by the executing florist.

There were always some orders that hadn't been accepted and we had to contact the florist and ask if they had a problem. Usually they would say that it was all in hand but they were so frantically busy they hadn't yet had a chance to update the order status. Unfortunately sometimes the response was along the lines of, "we are in a terrible mess, with more orders than we can handle and things are out of control".

I always felt sorry for any florist hit by unexpected staff absence on a peak day. I was always so grateful that our staff were so committed that they struggled in, even if they felt unwell. We all took the view that somehow, we just had to get in, no matter what. Nobody wanted to let the team down.

Handling complaints

It is a fact of life that every floristry business receives complaints from time to time. Some are justified and some are not. No matter how good your business is there will always be customers who don't like something about your products or your service.

You can get a bad reputation with an individual customer very easily. You may deliver a bouquet in mixed colours, because that is what the sender ordered, and then finds the recipient only likes pink. This will be your fault and the sender may vow never to use you again.

Some years ago, one recipient received several orders from us and complained about every single one for reasons that were quite bizarre. On one occasion, I visited her to show her an order form as proof that we had delivered precisely what the sender had specified. I explained that of all the hundreds of orders we had fulfilled on Mothering Sunday hers was the only complaint we had received. I even asked her in all honesty if she had some sort of grudge against us. In exasperation, we blacklisted her for a while and declined any orders for her. Then sometime later she did a complete volte-face and decided everything we did was marvellous.

I believe the floristry industry is extraordinarily understanding and generous in the way it handles complaints. The compensatory action taken is often way above what anyone would reasonably expect of other industries. Our motto was that if we had screwed up we would always do more than the customer expected to put things right. Sometimes this meant both refunding money and delivering replacement flowers.

However, I sometimes wonder if we roll over too easily. If you offer a no-quibble money back guarantee you can be taken for a mug.

Relay order complaints

We had one occasion when we received an Interflora order for an arrangement to be delivered to someone. Having made the arrangement and tried to deliver it we found that the recipient had moved to a different part of the country some months previously. Interflora asked us to cancel the order and resend it to another florist. So we received no payment despite the fact that one of our staff had spent twenty minutes making the arrangement. We wasted time and fuel and were unable to reuse the flowers because the stems had been cut short and we had no other orders for similar arrangements. So we lost money through no fault of our own and this is what you have to accept.

Situations like this make florists seethe but in fairness, in other similar situations, Interflora at least agreed to share the pain and gave us some compensation. I am told by a number of florists that this is rarely the case now. People tell me that their relay provider just accepts the customers word in the event of a complaint, cancels the order and the florist has to swallow it.

The different relay services each have their own views on how best to handle complaints and take the appropriate action. The above example is typical of what happens when a recipient has moved house, is away on holiday or has perhaps been discharged from hospital and does not live locally. Although it may seem very unfair, situations like this have to be considered as part of the perils of trading. However, I can't think of another industry that would give a full refund for something that had been custom made to the customer's specification and transported to the delivery address they have given.

Some say that as florists we have to take the wider view. Situations like this are bound to happen from time to time, but if we penalise the customer then people will be put off sending flowers at all. Their view is that it is better to accept the occasional written-off order and treat it as part of the overheads of your business.

My view is that the least we should do is explain the situation to the customer and try to agree a partial refund. For local orders customers are unlikely to baulk at this. People will often apologise, say that it was no fault of ours and that a 50 per cent refund is more than fair.

I once called a customer after we had tried to deliver flowers to a friend of his who had been discharged from hospital earlier that day. Before I could even talk about what we should do he solved the problem for me, saying that he realised it was not our fault and that the order should simply be cancelled and he didn't expect a refund.

It can be very frustrating when you feel that the person handling a complaint within a relay organisation has simply caved in and given the customer a full refund when it is not warranted. It is easy to take this view when you are an employee working for a large organisation but the poor old florist takes the financial hit, even if they are 100 per cent blameless.

Interflora used to listen to both sides of the argument and try to reach a compromise which everyone felt was fair. Many florists tell me this is no longer the case and now they take the hit nearly every time.

I had to investigate one complaint of non-delivery made by an Interflora customer. She had ordered a vase of flowers and a balloon for her son to be delivered to the porter's lodge at a Cambridge college and complained that we had not done this.

I knew I had delivered them myself so I returned to the college to find out what had happened. As I walked in I saw the flowers on the reception desk, exactly where I had left them. The porters said it was just the normal problem of a student not checking to see if there was any mail or a delivery for them – as they are repeatedly told to do at least once a day.

I phoned Interflora to tell them and subsequently found that they had given this lady a full refund. Interflora compensated us but I was still furious that they had backed down when we had done nothing wrong. The order was correctly made and delivered but the customer had bullied Interflora into a refund when the only person at fault was her son. This sort of 'customer care' is just stupid and encourages customers to try their luck.

It is all very well for a relay organisation to offer 'no quibble' guarantees but there are plenty of people out there who see this as an opportunity to get something for nothing when really there is zero cause for complaint.

No quibble guarantees can really hit the small retailer hard. Giving occasional refunds for a £25 gift wrap is no great problem, but at Valentines we frequently delivered huge bouquets of ten dozen top grade, grand prix roses costing well over £300. Giving a full refund on one of those would be a huge financial hit.

Assessing complaints

Every florist will receive some complaints – some will be valid and some won't. Some flowers will not last as long as they should and florists make mistakes, just like anyone else.

Almost every florist will quickly replace flowers, or give a refund, where the complaint is valid. If a regular customer told us their flowers only lasted a few days we would not even ask to see them. We would apologise and quickly deliver replacements. If the customer wasn't known to us and made a complaint regarding quality we would want to see just what was wrong before replacing them.

There are very good reasons for wanting to see the flowers first. Once a customer complained that, against her wishes, we had included roses in her bouquet, but when we saw it they were in

247

fact lisianthus. Another customer complained that we had not included carnations but it turned out he simply didn't know what carnations looked like.

Some florists take the view that the most cost-effective approach is to spend as little time as possible assessing the validity of a complaint. It is better to apologise and either refund or replace. There is some sense in this but personally I have always had a problem with lying down and letting someone walk all over you.

If we had really screwed up we gave a refund and replacement and a fulsome apology. If the complaint was a shameless try-on we gave them nothing at all.

Following one complaint of non-delivery, of an order some five weeks previously, I visited the house with replacement flowers. When I got there, I recognised both the house and the recipients. I then remembered very clearly that when I made the delivery they were sitting in their garden having a drink with friends. I explained this and even described their friends. They were extremely embarrassed and apologised profusely. I took the replacement flowers back to the shop!

Complaints of poor value can be very subjective. If you have listed and costed the flower content on the order form you can usually satisfy yourself whether or not the florist doing the make-up has made a mistake. Usually the content and costings prove correct. The problem is often that the customer has an unrealistic perception of what to expect for the money or perhaps flower prices were unusually high that week.

Most people will understand why prices are higher at Valentines or Mothering Sunday, but prices at the Dutch auctions can go sky high, for reasons quite unconnected with the UK. Customers don't want to know that it was Mother's Day in Russia!

It is not a good idea to tell the customer the total flower value that should have gone into their order. They will not want to know that you also had to pay the florist to make it, cover all the many costs of your business and try to make a little profit. The only people who can demand to know the actual flower value is Trading Standards, if a complaint has been referred to them. As they fully understand all the other costs involved this isn't usually a problem.

We only ever had two complaints referred to Trading Standards and on both occasions I found them to be totally understanding and supportive of our position. One of these complaints was from a lady who bought a large glass vase from us and said that it developed a crack, after she'd had it for three months. Our supplier was adamant this could only have happened if it had perhaps been in a dishwasher or had been knocked over. The lady was adamant she wanted a full refund so I contacted Trading Standards for advice. They responded by saying they were amazed we had received such a complaint and they would not expect us to make any refund.

Sometimes a recipient might ask the price of an item delivered to them, perhaps because they want to assess its value for money. This should never be divulged as it could upset the sender and it is obviously not ethical to divulge what someone has spent on a gift. If the recipient is really insistent, tell them to contact the sender.

A small inexpensive gift wrap is far more likely to generate a complaint than a large hand-tied or arrangement. Many recipients feel sure their friend or relative will have spent a lot of money on them and if they receive a basic bouquet they are more likely to be disappointed. This is yet another reason for developing high value sales. As well as boosting your profits they reduce the level of complaints.

Delivery problems

Most florists will find a neighbour who is willing to accept a delivery if the recipient is not at home but this can occasionally lead to problems. Many neighbours are only too pleased to help and will offer to put them in water or put them somewhere cool. However, some will refuse and tell you they wouldn't do anything to help their neighbour. One chap told me he wouldn't give the woman next door 'the steam off a rice pudding'!

I tried to deliver flowers to one address and had to visit the neighbour. The door was opened by a very friendly lady who said she was delighted to help. I left the flowers with her and put a card through the recipient's door. She later called the shop saying she refused to collect her flowers from 'that awful woman' and for all she cared the flowers could rot. Luckily the neighbour took the flowers round herself when she realised they were not going to be collected.

Another very angry lady complained that we had left her flowers at the house opposite and she did not know the people. She refused to cross the road and wanted me to return there immediately – a round trip of 12 miles – and redeliver. It was at the end of a long day and I simply refused and quite frankly didn't care if we lost this customer!

Another complaint was from someone whose Valentines flowers were delivered by a plain white van. They had expected one of our beautifully sign-written vans. They seemed amazed that we needed extra vans just for Valentines Day.

Despite these occasional delivery problems, I would always advocate finding a neighbour to leave an order with, rather than returning it to the shop. There are occasional exceptions, when perhaps the neighbour thinks the recipient is away on holiday. My experience is that returning any order to the shop for redelivery some time later is very expensive and time wasting.

Complaints about short product life

One of the most common complaints for any florist is that the flowers supplied did not last long. This may or may not be valid and, as I mentioned before, it is generally a good idea to see the flowers for yourself. Try to determine just what has happened to them. The problem may be due to poor quality, or to something the recipient has, or has not done.

It is impossible to state that a certain type of flower will last a certain length of time because flower life depends on so many variables. When you purchase flowers from a wholesaler you do not know when they were cut or what sort of conditions they have been kept in.

If they were fresh stock, bought at auction and promptly loaded into a refrigerated lorry, that delivered them promptly to you, then the flower life should be very good. But some wholesalers will decide that old unsold stock still looks pretty good a week later and they try to offload it on to some unsuspecting customer.

Most customers have no idea that their vases may contain bacteria or salt deposits from their dishwasher. When any of our customers complained that their flowers had quickly died we would replace them but ask the customer to bleach and thoroughly rinse their vases.

Some complaints are of course completely ridiculous. I remember delivering a gift wrap to a young couple and then making a further delivery a couple of days later. When I made the second delivery I saw that the bouquet I had delivered two days previously was propped up against a hot radiator in their hallway, still out of water! Any flowers treated with this sort of neglect will never last long.

Deliveries and complaint handling – checklist

- Create delivery sheets and file them afterwards
- Log 'precise' delivery times
- Train your drivers in the optimum way to make a delivery
- Minimise returns of deliveries by utilising neighbours
- Calculate your delivery charges very carefully
- Don't give away 'free' delivery
- Plan your peak period delivery areas carefully
- Check that outgoing relay orders are accepted and delivered
- Assess complaints fairly and reasonably
- When you get it wrong always do more to remedy the situation than the customer is expecting
- Check flower condition and try to establish what has happened to them since delivery
- Don't cave in to ridiculous complaints and get taken for a mug

Conclusion

I hope you have found this book useful. We have tried to be pragmatic about the current state of this fascinating industry.

It is unlikely that anyone who thinks that retail floristry is just about playing with flowers will make a living in this industry. It is very hard work and involves both creativity and business awareness to have any hope of being successful.

We have tried to spell out the reality of the floristry trade without painting an overly rosy picture. Whilst it undoubtedly presents some wonderful opportunities for a very fulfilling career, any new entrant needs to understand just what they are getting into.

After writing Buying and Running a Florist Shop one of my most pleasing reviews was in the Sunday Telegraph. They said the book would deter a lot of people, who really weren't cut out for this industry, from wasting their time and money. I like to think that I have stopped some people from wasting their hard-earned savings or a redundancy payment.

I am writing this the day after attending the 2017 Hampton Court Flower Show. Huge numbers of people with an absolute passion for everything to do with flowers attended. I came home last night totally enthused about the opportunities that do exist. It convinced me that there will continue to be many avenues open to the florists of the future.

Floristry is a lovely industry and for those who succeed it can provide an extremely enjoyable and rewarding way of life. Good luck!

Printed in Great Britain
by Amazon